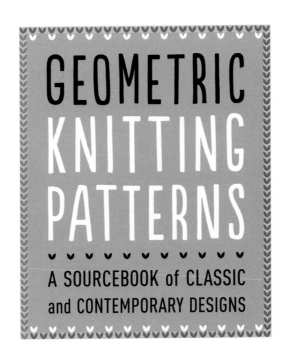

GEOMETRIC
KNITTING
PATTERNS

A SOURCEBOOK of CLASSIC
and CONTEMPORARY DESIGNS

First published in the UK in 2015 by
Apple Press
74–77 White Lion Street
London N1 9PH

www.apple-press.com

ISBN: 978 1 84543 586 8

Conceived, designed and produced by
Quid Publishing
Part of The Quarto Group
Level 4, Sheridan House
114 Western Road
Hove BN3 1DD
England

Design by Lyndsey Harwood

Printed in China

10 9 8 7 6 5 4 3 2 1

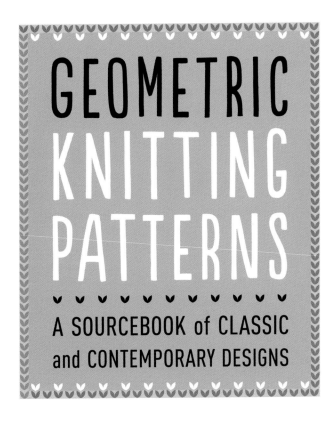

GEOMETRIC KNITTING PATTERNS

A SOURCEBOOK of CLASSIC and CONTEMPORARY DESIGNS

TINA BARRETT

APPLE

CONTENTS

INTRODUCTION

When I was approached to write this book, I thought it would prove an interesting design challenge and indeed it did. You would imagine that after 750-plus charts the whole theme of geometric knitting would be exhausted but alas, I fear this book only scratches the surface. This whole project has been a joy, and during the process my own knitting knowledge and technique have been expanded and tested, proving that one never stops learning. This is probably one of the many factors that make knitting such an absorbing and addictive craft.

At school, maths and geometry were definitely not my strong points, but I have always admired the aesthetic of bold angles, blocks of colour and architectural geometry. Researching this book has bridged a huge learning chasm that my poor maths teacher never could. I have marvelled at the myriad ways a square, triangle or pentagon can interlock, stand alone or stack together with other shapes to change and transform a particular pattern. Tessellating shapes fit together in almost magic eye proportions while shards of diamonds burst out from the page like a comet blast. The possibilities of geometry, it seems, are almost infinite.

For Chapter 5, I researched nature, which, although seemingly random, turns out to be hugely dominated by mathematical rules, fractals and sequences. Take for instance, the daisy, dahlia and rose; in appearance they are so different from each other yet they all follow nature's same Golden Rules.

In art and culture worldwide, geometric shapes are favoured and repeated throughout history, some trying to capture the shapes of nature, like the Norwegian rose and snowflake motifs, while others, like the Celtic spirals and knots, aim to depict bigger themes such as the circle of life and the eternal cycle of the seasons.

Fashion has also seized on geometry to make a statement. The 1920s and 30s Art Nouveau and Art Deco movements took bold shapes and blocks of colour to create abstract geometry and make a statement. Wallpaper, paintings and fabric were chic in monochrome or daringly avant-garde in golds, reds, turquoises and greens. In the 1960s, Mary Quant ruled with geometric monochrome print dresses and Pucci sported tessellated circles and paisley motifs in eye-watering brights.

So you see, throughout history, geometric patterns have rocked the world and if you think they aren't your thing, I assure you this book will prove you wrong. Turn the pages and you will undoubtedly find a chart crying out to be knitted into a sweater, an afghan or a cushion cover. The patterns on these pages are just a starting point, created for you to use in your own particular creative way. Mix them up, change the colourway, add some beads, embroider over the top, or even try combining several in one project. Whatever you choose, I really hope this book and its geometry inspires and informs your next knitting project the way it has now inspired my craft.

Happy knitting!

Tina B xxxx

HOW TO USE THIS BOOK

This book has been designed as a source book of geometric knitting charts that will inspire and enhance your own particular knitting projects. However, when one takes the lid off a box of mouth-watering luxury chocolates, the choice can be a bit daunting and you might not quite know where to start. It may well be the same when using this book. With over 750 charts to choose from, how on earth does one begin?

Exactly for this reason, I have divided the book into easy-to-use chapters such as stripes, chevrons, motifs, etc. If your project is simply crying out for a stripe or check, then these particular chapters will logically be your first port of call. But from here, I have explored further on your behalf and tried to develop each idea fully within this section. For instance, the stripes chapter may well begin with simple stripes. This is perfectly fine if you need a simple, effective stripe pattern for your project, but I have delved deeper and suggested additional exploration of this theme. There are not only simple stripes, but also textured, broken, short row and even Fair Isle stripes to choose from. In addition, I push you even further, asking you to look at different ways you can use the chart pattern. It may be that knitting in beads or adding Swiss darning could enhance the look of your work, or you can use a different combination of yarn textures such as angora and merino.

Depending on your skill as a knitter, you will find some of these charts easier to work than others. Colour knitting is an important skill that is very useful to have in your knitting armoury, as it can really turn your finished work into a masterpiece. For beginners, I suggest sticking to Fair Isle style charts, i.e. those with only two colours used either all-over or in every row. For these charts, you will need to use the stranding technique and you will find all the technical instructions for learning this on page 239.

For those knitters with a little more experience, why not try a spot of intarsia? Perhaps the prospect of all those bobbins and balls of yarn tangling together seems a bit daunting, but I assure you, it's almost like baking a cake. First, thoroughly read the recipe, or in this case the chart, and take in what you need to do. Then gather your ingredients, i.e. wind the bobbins of individual coloured yarn you'll need. Finally, bake, or knit, the work. When ready, you can smooth out the lumps of a cake with frosting. Practice will make perfect. All the technical instructions for intarsia can be found on page 236.

But then, for the more daring and experimental knitters I have suggested adorning and enhancing your work with beads, sequins, embroidery and Swiss darning. If you have never attempted any of these techniques, I really urge you to try. Read the technical instructions on pages 241 and 249 and start experimenting. There is no such thing as a mistake. In all my years as a knitter, I've often found that trying a new technique helps develop creativity. It will surprise and delight you how wonderful and stylish an artfully knitted-in bead can look.

As a final word of encouragement, I also urge you to use colour. Try to mix up your palette and really play with how colour choice can affect the finished look of the knitted pattern. Light and darks can dominate or recede, altering the aesthetic of the chart entirely. Use different textures of yarn against each other and take the chance to experiment. All the charts are developed to be the ideal swatch size. Knit up the same chart several times using a variety of colours, yarns, beads and embroidery before deciding on which you will incorporate in your chosen project. You will find that most works of genius are a by-product of a happy accident.

However, all these wonderful patterns do require you to read from a knitting chart. If you have never ever done this before, then here's how.

HOW TO READ A KNITTING CHART

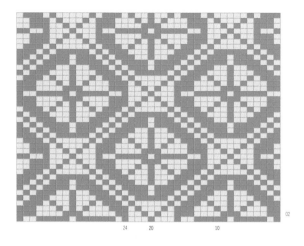

24   20   10   02

Key
- ☐ RS: Knit WS: Purl
- ■ Custom 1
- ▨ Custom 2

This is a typical example of a knitting chart found in this book. As you can see, it has a key beside it that shows the colours of yarn used. For this book, I have used a palette of 24 colours to make things easier, but you can either follow my lead, in which case the yarns and their colours are listed on page 253, or you can experiment with your own. Bear in mind that when you substitute yarn, you will need to refer to the ball band for the needle size required and tension details. For this book, we have used a DK weight yarn that required 4.5 mm (US size 7) needles and was knit to a tension of 20 sts x 25 rows over 10 cm (4in) using stocking stitch.

As you can see, there is a row of numbers along the bottom horizontal row of the chart. These represent the stitch numbers. The numbers running vertically up the right-hand side of the chart represent row numbers. Those numbers highlighted in red show the number of rows and stitches in each repeat. This is a handy guide if you want to insert that repeat into a project that is not the same size as the chart. You could photocopy and enlarge the chart for ease of use.

To work the chart, first cast on the amount of stitches required, i.e. the total number listed across the horizontal row. Begin working Row 1 and every odd numbered row from right to left, changing colours when required. In colour work, this will be a knit row.

When you have finished the row, turn your work so the wrong side is facing and read Row 2 and all even-numbered rows from left to right. This row will be a purl row, so work the row as shown, changing colour when required. Work all the rows from the chart until they are complete.

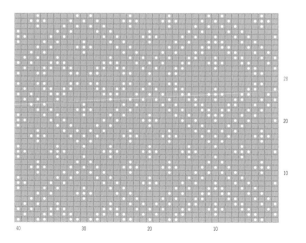

28   20   10

40   30   20   10

Key
- ☐ RS: Knit WS: Purl
- ▨ Azure
- ▣ RS: Purl WS: Knit

Some charts will have a slightly different key. Instead of identifying the colours you will need, it shows the stitch type required. For instance, this chart tells you that when you come to the stitch with a dot in it, you will be purling it on a right side row and knitting it on a wrong side row. Otherwise, the chart is read in exactly the same way as the colour chart shown. It merely shows the change of stitch and forms the pattern with texture instead of colour.

STRIPES

The easiest form of colour knitting, simple stripes are well within the ability of the novice knitter. But, master knitters shouldn't look down on stripes – at their most complex, stripes can challenge the skills of the best colour knitters. Because of the nature of stripe patterns, most of the charts in this chapter do not have marked-out repeats, but the pattern is set and you can either write out or graph out the repeats to the size of the knitted fabric you need.

HORIZONTAL STRIPES

The absolutely simple-to-knit, classic horizontal stripe doesn't date, and can offer more than meets the eye depending on the techniques you use to work it and, of course, the colours you choose: chart 5 is a simple pattern, but the riot of colours makes a bold statement.

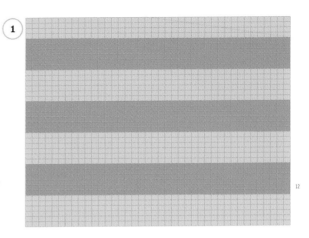

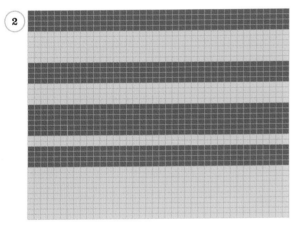

▼ *If you work single-row stripes on conventional straight knitting needles, then you have to either calculate the number of rows between stripes carefully so that the yarn is at the right end when you need it, or you have to break the yarn and darn in the ends of every row. But if you work back and forth on a circular needle (or a double-pointed needle if it's a small piece of knitting), then you just slide the knitting to the right end to pick up the yarn as you need it. Don't forget to catch in the yarn not in use at the end of every row.*

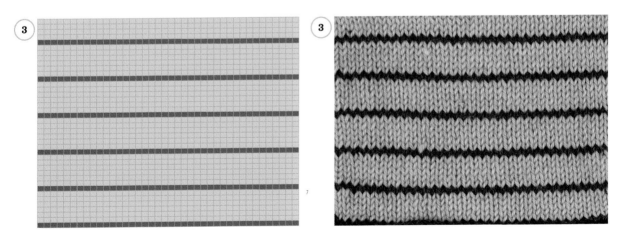

4

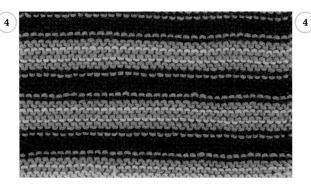

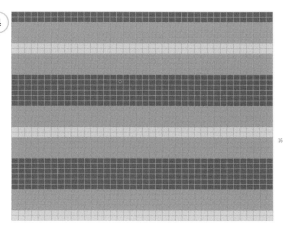

▲ *Knitting a stripe pattern in garter stitch can give you extra stripes where the colours overlap, depending on the row count of each stripe. But do remember that garter stitch knits up shorter than stocking stitch, which is the stitch size that these charts were drawn for.*

5

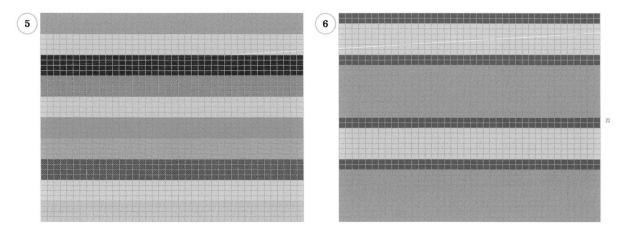

6

7

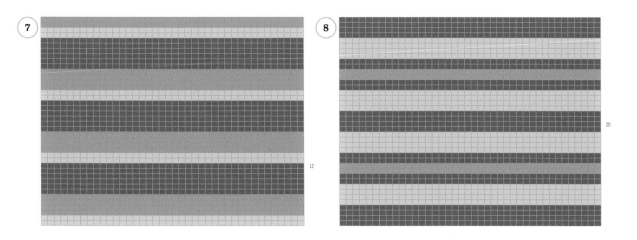

8

VERTICAL AND DIAGONAL STRIPES

Both these types of stripe need colourwork techniques: intarsia (see page 236) for wide stripes, or stranding (see page 239) for narrow or diagonal stripes. You can simply turn the pattern sideways and knit the stripes horizontally (so they'll be vertical on the knitting), but remember that a stitch is wider than it is tall, so you may need to adjust both rows and stitches.

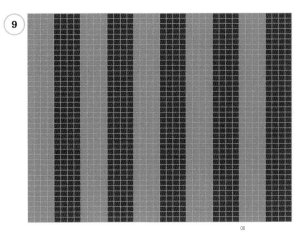

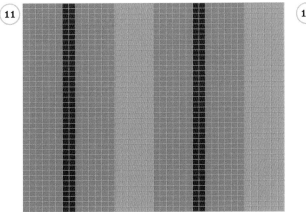

▲ One way of avoiding having to work colour knitting is to use beading (see page 249) or embroidery (see page 241) to create vertical stripes. Here, the dark stripes are Swiss-darned onto the knitted fabric, and the beaded stripes use the knitting-in technique so that one bead can be placed above another on every row.

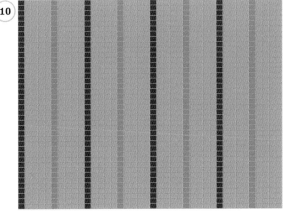

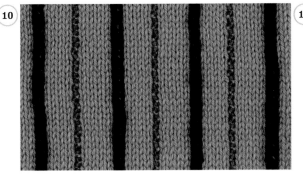

13

13

▲ *As a knitted stocking stitch is wider than it is tall, a regularly incremental diagonal, such as the one in chart 13, won't run at 45 degrees. This chart, which has an irregular – although repeated – diagonal, produces a stripe that's much closer to 45 degrees.*

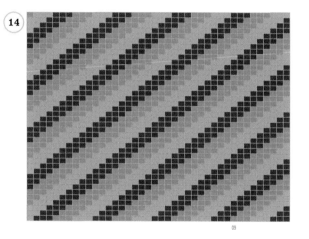

14

09

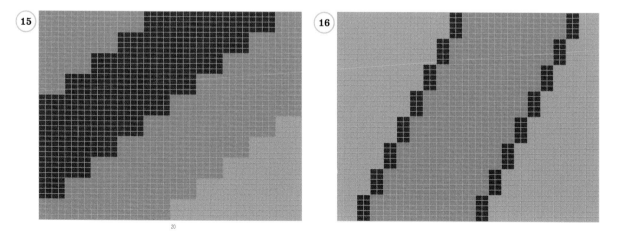

15

20

16

TEXTURE STRIPES

Texture patterns can be written out or given as charts, and knitters tend to prefer one version or the other. If a pattern only gives the information in the version you dislike, then it can be well worth transcribing the repeat into your preferred style. Here there are charts, with a written version for the swatches.

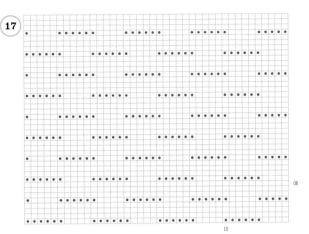

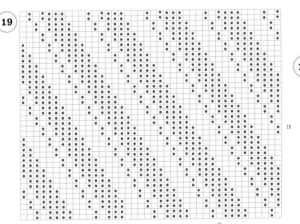

Key

▢ k on RS, p on WS
⦿ p on RS, k on WS
ⓥ inc to 3
⚠ p3tog

▼ **Row 1 (RS):** [K1, p1, k3, p4] to end.
Row 2 and every alt row: Purl the stitches that were knitted, knit the stitches that were purled.
Row 3: [P1, k1, p1, k3, p3] to end.
Row 5: [P2, k1, p1, k3, p2] to end.
Row 7: [P3, k1, p1, k3, p1] to end.
Row 9: [P4, k1, p1, k3] to end.
Row 11: [K1, p4, k1, p1, k2] to end.
Row 13: [K2, p4, k1, p1, k1] to end.
Row 15: [K3 p4, k1, p1] to end.
Row 17: [P1, k3, p4, k1] to end.
Row 18: Purl the stitches that were knitted, knit the stitches that were purled.
Rows 1–18 set pattern.

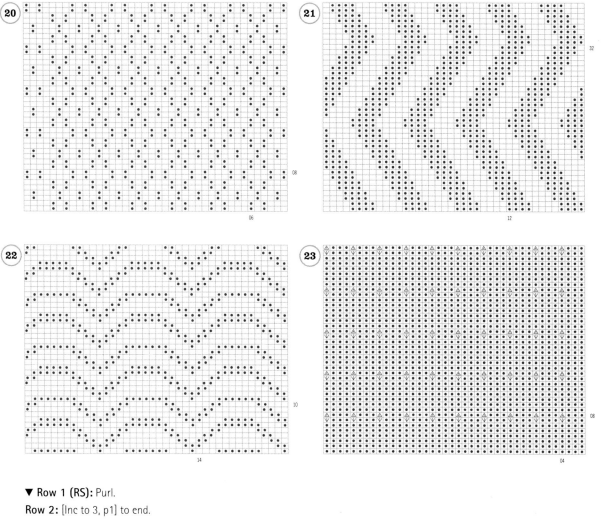

▼ **Row 1 (RS):** Purl.

Row 2: [Inc to 3, p1] to end.

Row 3: [K3, p1] to end.

Row 4: [P3tog, p1] to end.

Row 5: Purl.

Row 6: [P1, inc to 3] to end.

Row 7: [P1, k3] to end.

Row 8: [P1, inc to 3] to end.

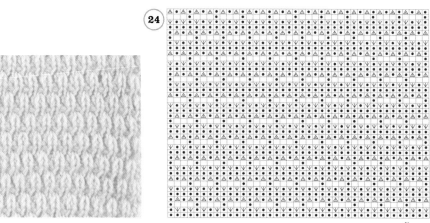

BROKEN STRIPES

Make more of the basic horizontal stripe by putting breaks into it, and then take that idea further still by adding shapes to stripes, or changing the angles of stripes. You can use details like these in combination with plain stripes to add another dimension to an essentially simple design.

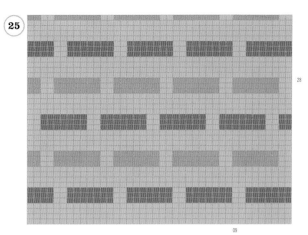

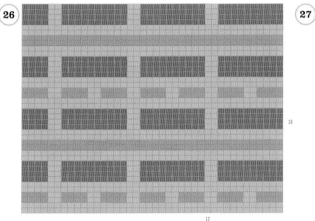

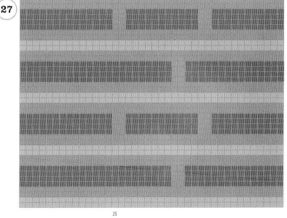

▼ To work a break in a stripe, join in a new length of the break-colour yarn (here, the darker colour) as for intarsia knitting (see page 236), and strand (see page 239) the other yarn across the back of it. Darn the ends in afterwards. Working like this means that there is minimal stranding to deal with, though depending on the number of breaks you have, there can be a lot of ends to darn in.

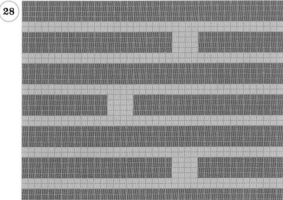

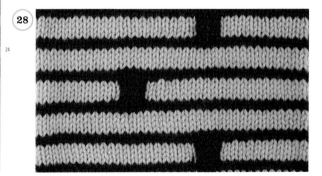

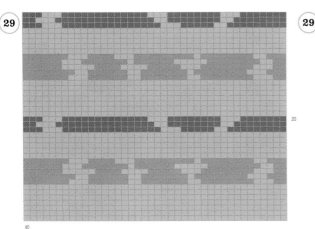

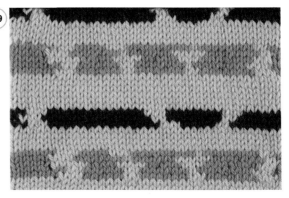

▲ These broken stripes are stranded across the stripe rows. You need to be very careful to keep the stranding tension even and not too tight on the stripe rows, or they will look puckered in comparison to the plain rows. One stripe in this style can look very effective in an otherwise unbroken stripe pattern.

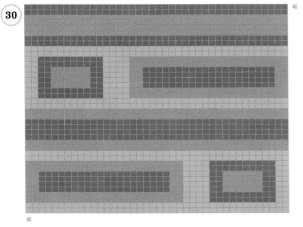

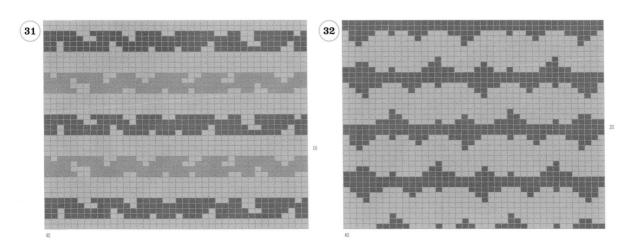

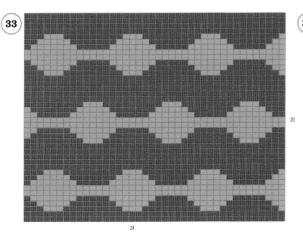

33

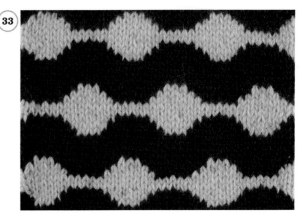

33

▲ These narrow 2-row stripes have had circles added to them, reminiscent of a string of beads. The chart shows this as a repeat design, with the beads staggered, but you could work a single row of beads, or repeat the same row so that the beads line up vertically. The background of this swatch is worked in a smooth yarn and the beads in a mohair (used tripled to match the weight of the smooth yarn), to add texture as well as pattern.

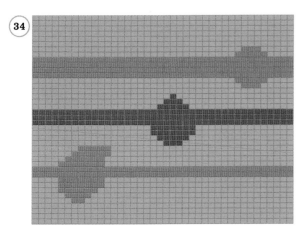

34

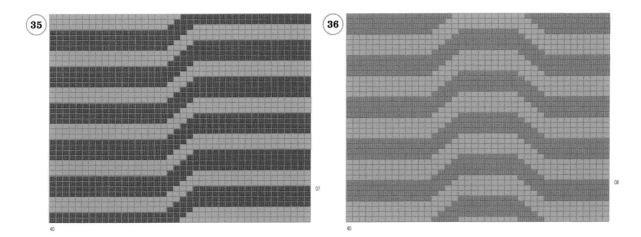

35

36

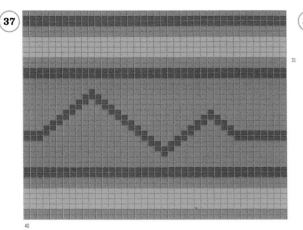

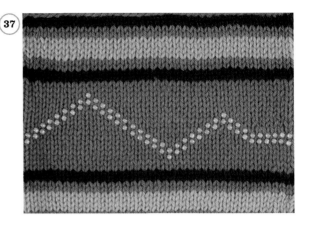

▲ *Beads are a quick and effective way of adding texture and detail to a design, and they work very well in stripe patterns. Here, the beads are knitted in so that they lie at an angle that complements the zigzag in the stripe pattern. On straight stripes, slip stitch beading (see page 249) is equally effective. One irregular stripe in a pattern of straight horizontal stripes can look very effective, whether it's worked in yarn or beads.*

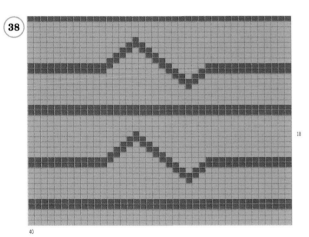

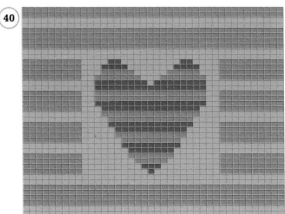

SHORT-ROW EFFECT STRIPES

These patterns are based on the way short-row shaping works – where rows are turned before the end – but they are worked straight across the row. This is the complicated end of the stripe spectrum. These charts don't have repeats, so to use them over larger pieces of knitting you will need to graph them out, following the pattern as set radiating out from the midpoint.

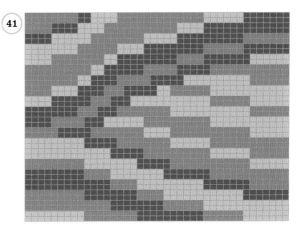

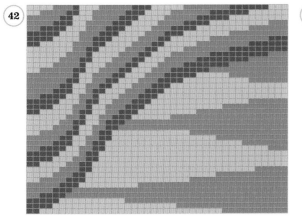

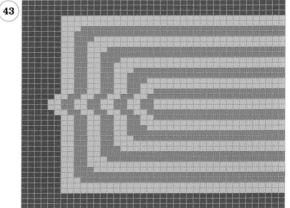

▼ *Complex, multi-coloured stripe patterns like this are best worked back and forth on a circular needle (or a double-pointed needle if it's a small piece of knitting). This allows you to pick up yarns from either end of the row as works best, and saves you joining in and darning in the ends of lots of new colours.*

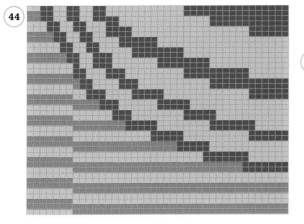

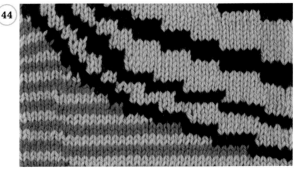

45

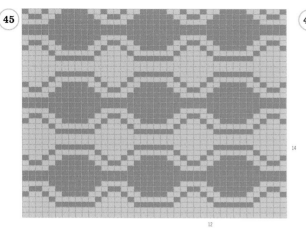

45

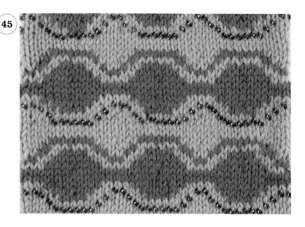

▲ *Beading (see page 249) is a flexible and versatile technique that can be used to add dimension, texture and embellishment to almost any design. Here, just one of the rows outlining the main motif is beaded; the other outlining row is stranded colourwork (see page 239).*

46

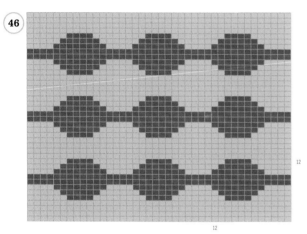

47

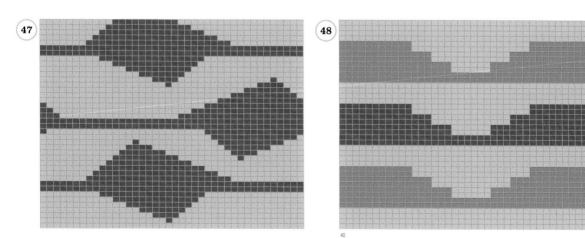

48

FAIR ISLE STRIPES

Strictly speaking, traditional Fair Isle patterns have just two colours in a single row, but there can be many colours in the whole pattern. These charts use just three colours each, but you could replace those colours differently to create much more multi-coloured results. You'll need to practise your stranding technique (see page 239) to work these patterns perfectly.

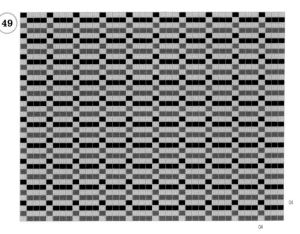

49

04

04

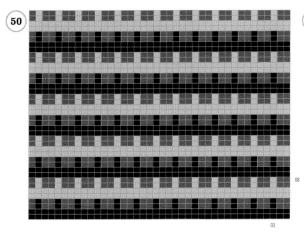

50

08

03

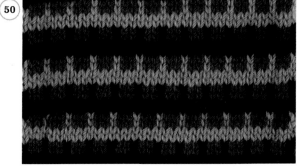

50

▲ *In working this swatch you will be carrying yarns up the side of the work as well as across it. It's a very small and simple repeat, but the colours you choose will make different elements of it dominant. Here, the dark and light stripes stand out, but if they were a neutral colour and the small squares were dark, the effect would be very different.*

51

04

04

52

06

07

53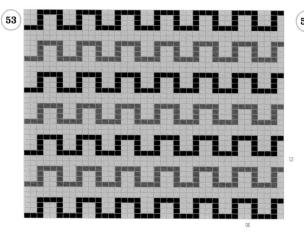

54

55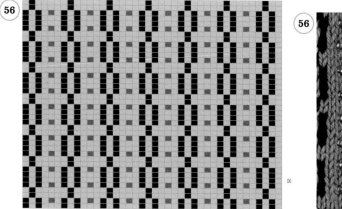

▼ Beads are a great way of adding an extra dimension to a Fair Isle pattern. The traditional single stitches of colour are easily replaced by a single bead. You can use the slip-stitch method (see page 249), as here, but be aware that the bead will hang at the bottom of the stitch.

56

56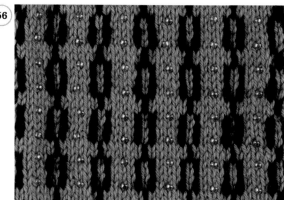

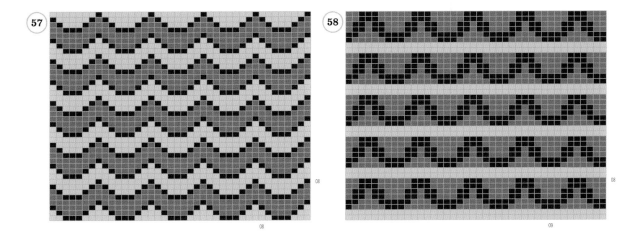

▼ Chart 60 creates a peculiar optical illusion because of the way the pattern is formed: the rectangles of the chart actually look as though they are distorted, though they are all entirely regular. The effect doesn't translate across to the knitting, which looks completely normal.

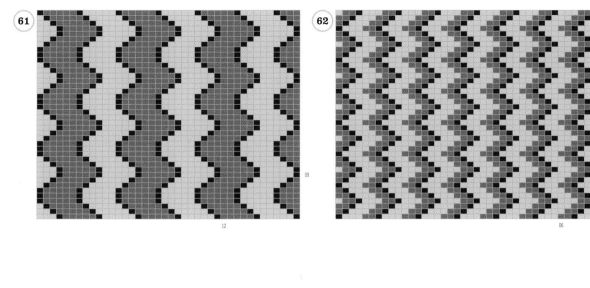

61 09 12

62 06 06

63 12 08

▼ This is a very traditional pattern, with just subtle changes to the patterned bands to create interest. The wide plain bands give you a respite from colour stranding for a few rows. It's always worth exploring and swatching traditional patterns in colourways you like, because the elegant simplicity of a lot of the designs really doesn't date.

64 17 13

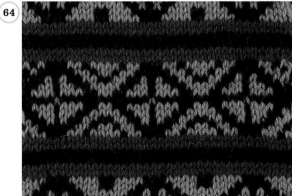

64

RADIATING STRIPES

As with the short-row effect patterns (see page 22), these charts don't have repeats, although the pattern is set and you can extend it by graphing or writing it out to suit the number of stitches in your piece of knitting.

▼ *If a pattern is bold and fairly simple, then knitting it with texture rather than colour can be an interesting and effective option. This swatch is worked in stocking stitch and reverse stocking stitch and the design shows up beautifully. However, more complex patterns can get rather lost if worked in texture.*

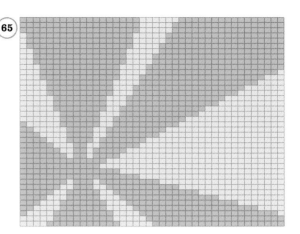

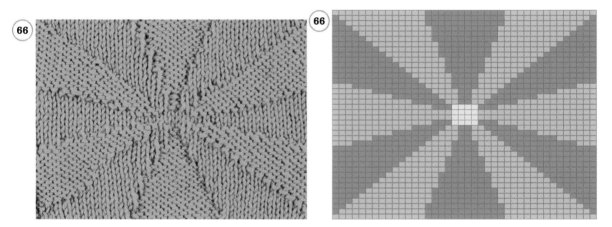

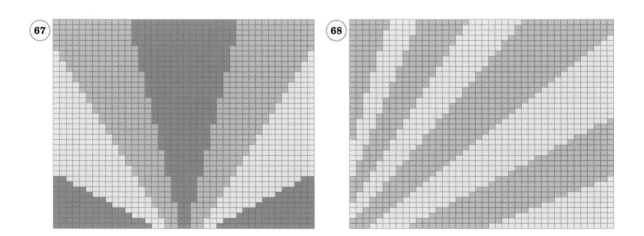

69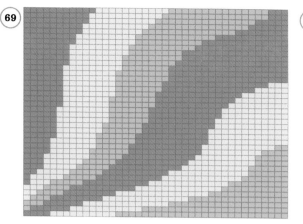

70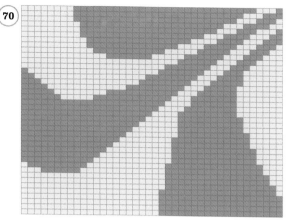

71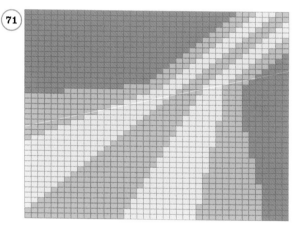

▼ *Another way of translating a colour knitting pattern is to embroider it onto plain knitted fabric. Here, the outlines of the shapes are Swiss darned (see page 241). Do be aware that embroidery will almost always affect the drape of knitted fabric; it will be stiffer and the embroidered sections can hang awkwardly if they are densely stitched.*

72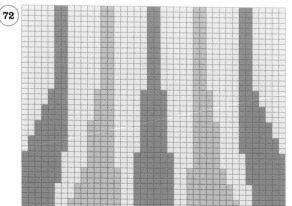

72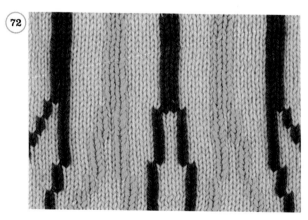

ABSTRACT STRIPES

Stripes can be twisted, bent, curved or cut to form a whole variety of abstract shapes, many of which can end up stepping quite a long way away from the original stripes that formed them. Some of these charts set a pattern you can follow to make them larger, while others would need a more intuitive approach to extend them. Be inspired by these designs and create your own abstract stripe patterns.

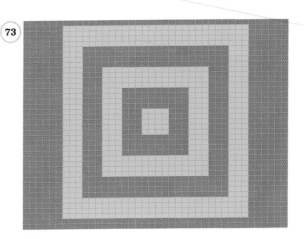

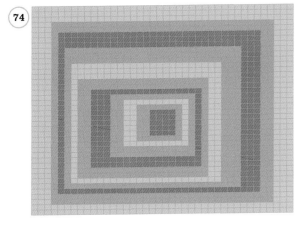

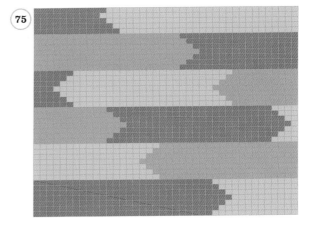

▼ *For a design like this target, you can strand (see page 239) across the back of the target area only; this will mean that area is a different thickness to the rest of the fabric, but it's a more efficient use of yarn. You can use both ends of a ball, the outer end and the centre pull end, to knit different areas of the pattern.*

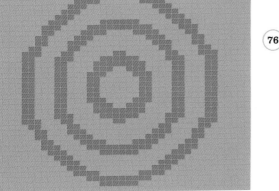

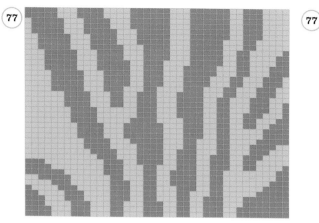

▲ *This is a good example of how more complex colour patterns can get lost if they are worked in texture. The chart is based on zebra stripes, and the bold contrast of the colours make it look clear and graphic. However, the subtlety of stitch texture softens edges and the clarity of the pattern is entirely lost here. If you want to work a colour pattern as texture, choose something simple and strong.*

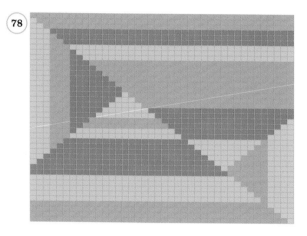

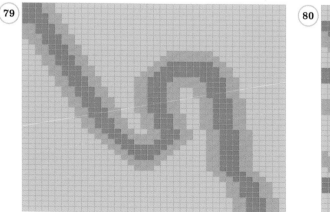

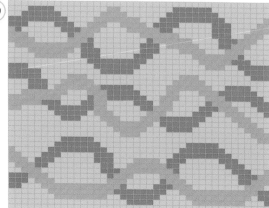

STRIPED
WALL ART

Create your own knitted 'painting' in your favourite
yarns and colours to complement your room scheme.
This is a very easy-to-make project that's great for
beginner knitters, and because it's quite small, it won't
take forever to finish.

YARNS
Regia Design Line Random Stripe: 1 × 50g (231
yds) ball in Snappy (02900) A
Anchor Artiste Metallic: 2 × 25g (109 yds) ball in
Shade 308 B
Rowan Pure Wool 4ply: 1 × 50g (1³/₄oz) ball in
Ochre (461) C

TOOLS
Pair of 2.75mm (US 2) knitting needles
Blunt tapestry needle
Canvas board measuring 20cm × 20cm (8 × 8in)
Fabric glue

TENSION
30 sts and 32 rows to 10cm (4in) using 2.75mm
(US 2) needles and measured over St st

MEASUREMENTS
20 × 20cm (8 × 8in)

ABBREVIATIONS
See page 252

WALL ART
Using yarn A, cast on 55 sts.
Row 1 (RS): Knit.
Row 2: Purl.
Rep rows 1–2, 3 times more.
Next row: Cast on 6 sts, k to end. (61 sts)
Next row: Cast on 6 sts, p to end. (67 sts)
Rep rows 1–2, 12 times.

STRIPE SEQUENCE
Knit 2 rows in B.
Knit 2 rows in C.
Knit 2 rows in A.
Rep last 6 rows 7 more times and then first 2 rows
once more.
Break yarns B and C.
Rep rows 1–2, 12 times.
Next row: Cast off 6 sts, k to end. (61 sts)
Next row: Cast off 6 sts, p to end. (55 sts)
Rep rows 1–2, 4 times.
Cast off.

FINISHING
Weave in any loose ends and block according to ball band
instructions.
On the WS, sew together row end and row edge ends at the
four corners. Fit knitted piece over canvas and glue into place
around the edges using fabric glue.

2

CHEVRONS

The classic zigzag striped chevron has long been a classic.
Knitwear designer Missoni reworked this favourite so many
times that it became the brand's signature. However, the
chevron shape can be so much more than this, and in the
following chapter, we explore the myriad ways it can be
used as a geometric pattern. From horizontals to verticals,
borders and motifs – there's a zigzag in here
for everyone.

HORIZONTAL

The chevron is one of the most widely recognised geometric shapes. Although it looks tricky, it's simpler than it looks to produce. If you have mastered stripes, then I would definitely suggest the chevron as the next step up. We'll begin this chapter by looking at horizontal chevrons.

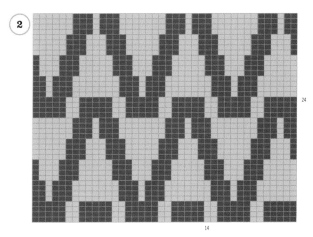

▼ If you are new to chevrons then try starting with this one. Using two colours only and wide bands between the chevron stripe, this chart is ideal for getting you used to knitting the zigzag shape and stranding the yarn. Try to keep the tension of your work even as you strand the accent colour along the back of the work. A tip for managing the tension is remembering to never work more than five stitches before twisting the yarns over each other.

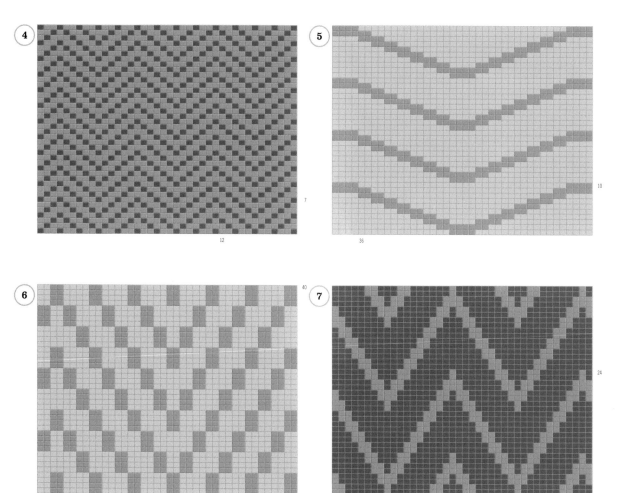

6   36

7   40   21   24

▼ By deepening the zigzag of the chevron, a much bolder shape is
achieved. Any colour goes here. Try retro monochrome, hot pink and
orange, or tone it down with neutral shades of mocha and cream.

8   40   18

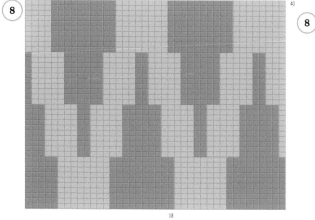

8

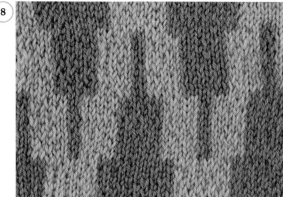

9

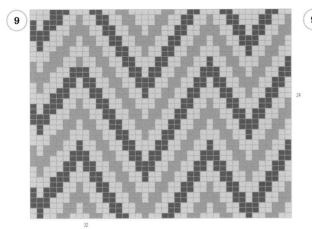

32 · 24

9

▲ *This chart shows the classic narrow zigzag chevron as made famous by Missoni. Here it is worked in three colours but really it is up to you exactly how many colours you choose to use. It's a perfect choice for cushion covers, afghans, scarves and rugs. Why not try a mix of sea greens, teals, cool blues and sand colours for a nautical feel or go autumnal with warm oranges, reds and browns?*

10

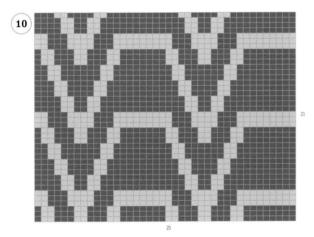

20 · 21

11

12

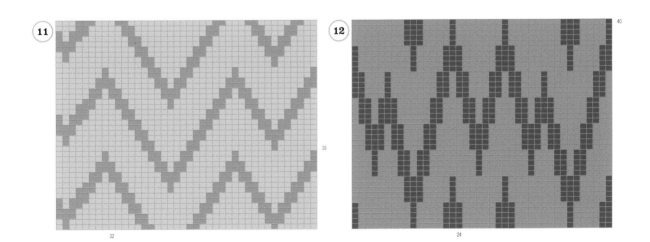

32 · 16 · 24 · 40

13

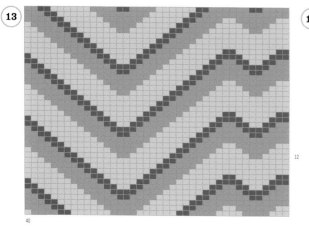

14

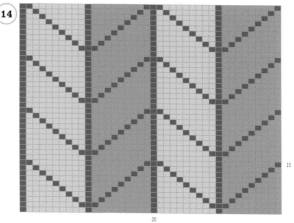

▲ *A chunkier, three-dimensional version of the chevron here. The darkest accent colour works a feather shape throughout the pattern. Try beading (see page 249) along the thin vertical stripes of this chart to add a bit of sparkle to the stem of the feather.*

15

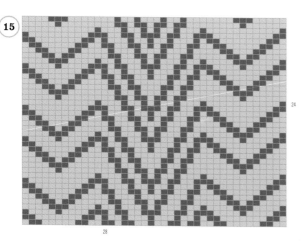

▼ *I love the way that clever use of the chevron shape almost suggests a heart shape at the lower part of the chart. You could use a third colour yarn to fill the centre of the heart to add further emphasis.*

16

16

VERTICAL

By merely altering the direction of the chevron from horizontal to vertical, see how the visual of the knitted work alters, making it appear longer and narrower than that of the horizontal ones. Back-to-back chevrons, flattened tops and varying widths also add an extra dimension here.

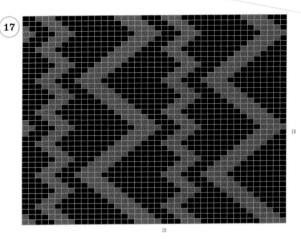

▼ *What happens when chevrons are used back to back? They form diamonds as shown on this chart – very reminiscent of some of the patterns used on golf socks and with a slight Argyle feel. If you are feeling bold, why not add a bobble to the centre of the diamond?*

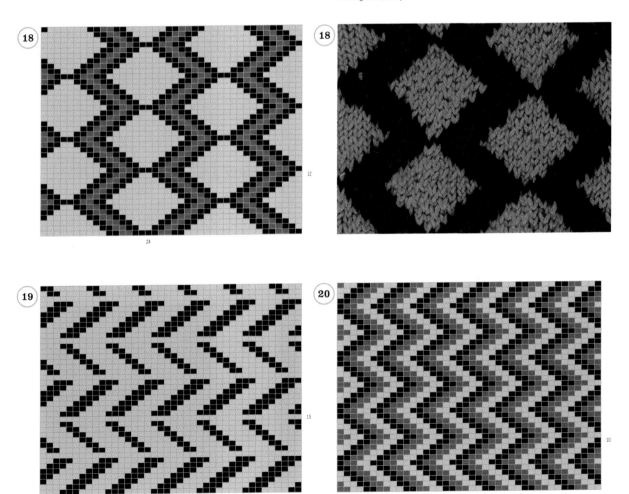

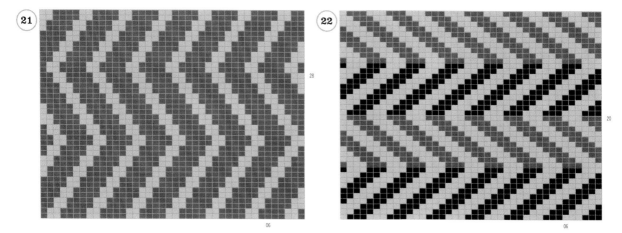

▼ *Just like Fair Isle, this striking chart uses only two colours in every row. There is a regular colour change every three stitches, which makes it a great introduction to stranded knitting (see page 239).*

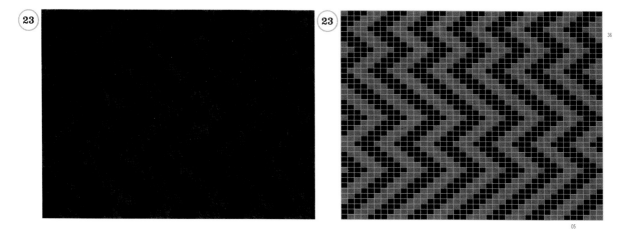

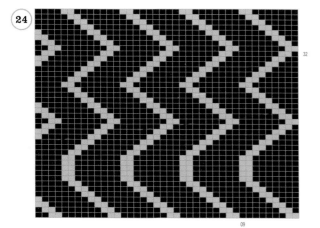

CHEVRON +

We've called this section Chevron +, and for good reason. These really are chevrons but not as you might have previously known them. Real fun has been had designing pared down, abstract, broken-up and faded-out chevrons. These playful chevrons will add a fun element to any knitted project.

25

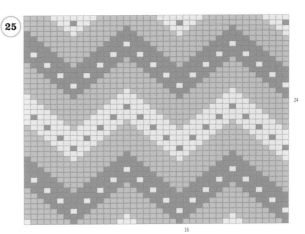

26

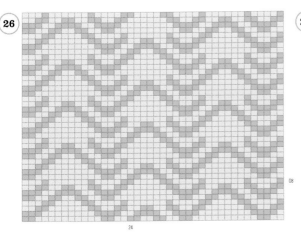

27

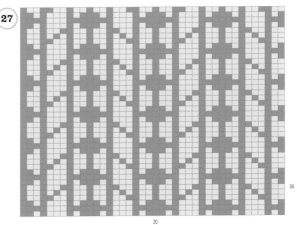

▼ *Hard to believe this is a chevron shape, but it is. A more complex chart, it takes a little added concentration to knit, but the bold aesthetic makes it a perfect choice for homeware items. This is a two-tone version of the classic Fair Isle OXO pattern.*

28

28

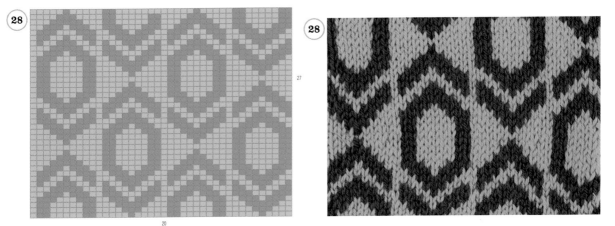

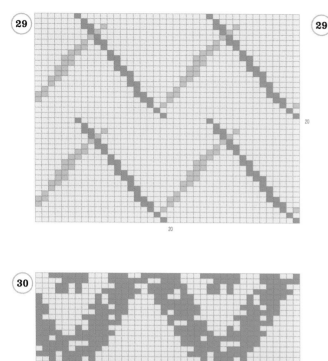

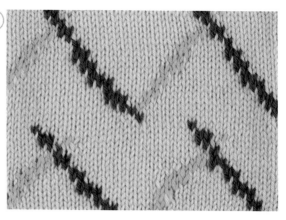

▲ *I love the way this chevron becomes an understated flick, as if drawn on casually with a felt-tip pen. Use small bobbins of yarn to work the mid- and dark blues here (see page 236). The area of colour is so small it is not worth stranding the yarn. Bobbins will make life far easier in this case.*

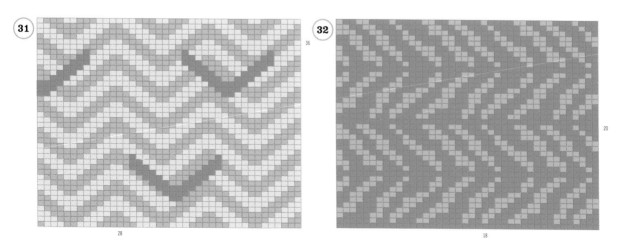

33

29

12

34

30

12

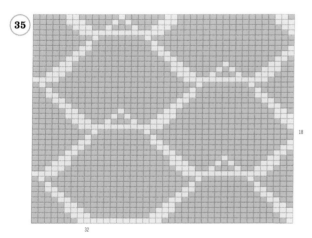

35

18

32

▼ *This bold vertical chevron reminds me of stonewashed jeans,*
especially when it's worked in these denim shades. The dark zigzag
fades out and shatters in places, softening the edges and giving a
'faded in the wash' feel. Use a bobbin of dark blue to work this chart
(see page 236), although it would be great worked in monochrome too.

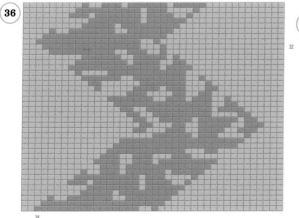

36

32

38

36

37

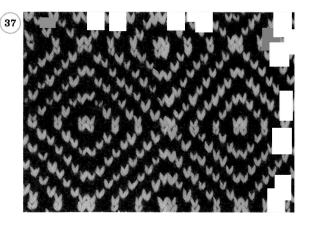

37

▲ *Reminiscent of an Andy Warhol original, a single pop-art chevron motif is echoed four times in two shades of the same blue. The combination of back-to-back chevrons and changing tonal values is mesmerising! A great chart for any retro project.*

38

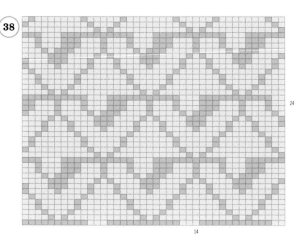

39

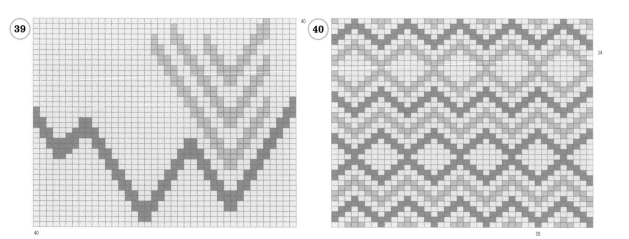

40

DIFFERENT SHAPES

This section explores chevrons in a much looser way. Some of the angles have relaxed into drooping curves and swags while others have become more cuboid and geometric. Have a look at how Chart 42 becomes almost ribbon-like when the chevron is twisted. This design would make a great border pattern if used as a single pattern repeat.

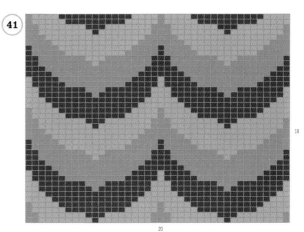

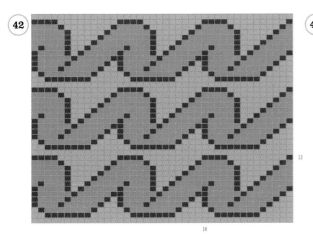

▼ What happens if you squeeze a feathered chevron pattern together? This is the result! The squeezed arrows become swag-like and chunky. Use bobbins (see page 236) for the dark and mid-tones but you will need to strand the lightest colour throughout the work. Take care to keep the tension even on this more complex knitting chart and try to avoid holes at the edges of the blocks of colour by twisting the two yarns around each other.

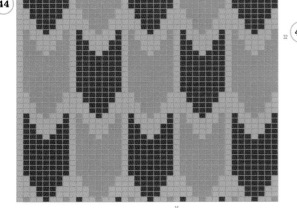

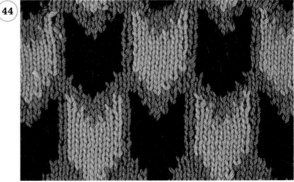

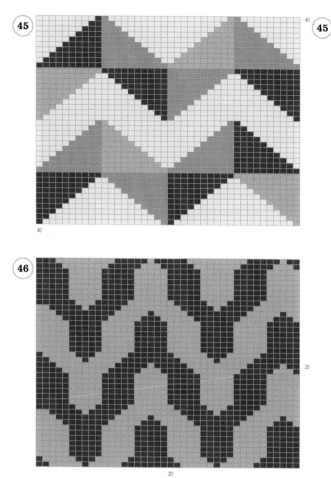

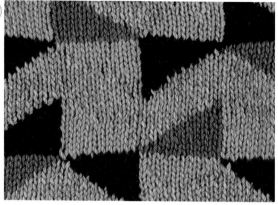

▲ *Chart 45 shows how clever use of colour can change a simple wide horizontal shape. By adding triangles of purples and lilacs to the band, the illusion becomes arrow-like. It echoes the geometry of a fabric quilt and therefore might be very effective worked in squares, then pieced together to make a bold knitted bedspread.*

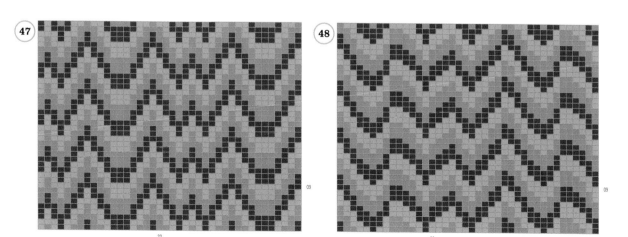

CHEVRONS AND COLOUR

I have long been interested in the combination of colours and how they draw the eye. Several of the designs on this page use harmonising colours that allow the chevrons to merge and blend tastefully together. In marked contrast, the others use bright, vibrant colours that really make the zigzags come alive and sing. Try wrapping different coloured yarns side by side along the length of a ruler to make a colour combination that suits you. Do you prefer a tasteful harmony of tones and shades or a symphony of clashing colours?

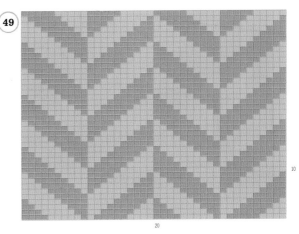

49

10

20

▼ *Three bold-coloured horizontal chevrons with the centre third pushed up just enough to misalign the regularity of the colours. Like a slot machine that has one of its cherries in the wrong place, this pattern makes for a quirky addition to any knitted item.*

50

39

30

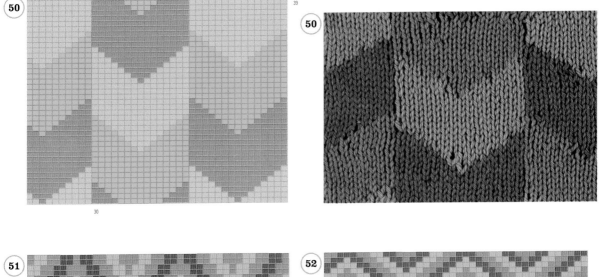

50

51

14

16

52

06

18

53

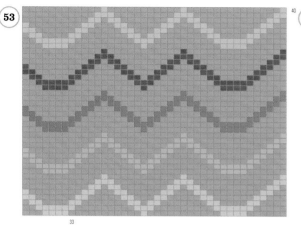

40

33

54

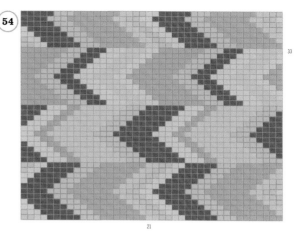

33

21

▼ A complex combination of vertical back-to-back zigzags worked in five colours – definitely a chart for the more experienced knitter. Worked in these shades, it suggests Native American culture. It's a stunning choice for afghans, rugs and cushion covers.

55

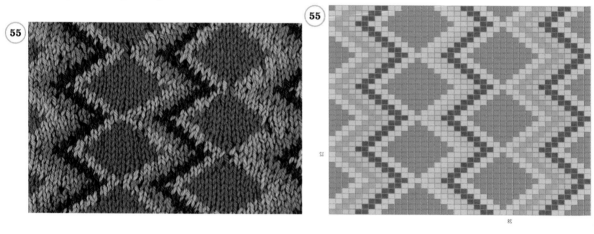

55

12

28

56

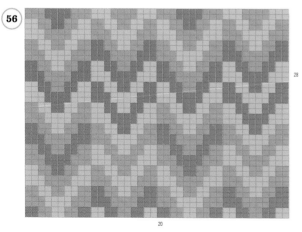

28

20

MOTIFS

This page contains some quick and handy motifs that are perfect for chevron fans who don't feel they can quite commit to a large colourwork project. Here you will find a chart that is smaller and easier to tackle. All you need do is select the ideal project to put it on to!

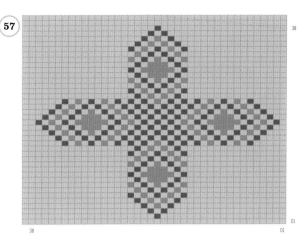

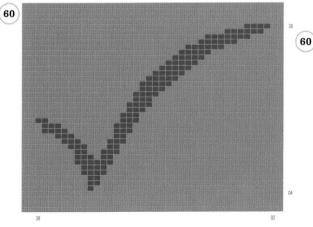

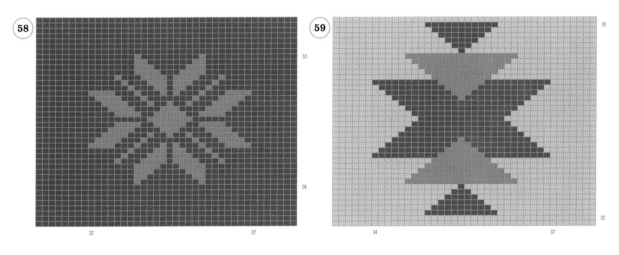

▼ This chart is the epitome of the deconstructed chevron motif. A mere tick like a teacher's mark across the knitting. Why not centre a large version of this chevron across the front of a shell top or slouchy sweater? It says thumbs up to the world, I'm 'A okay'!

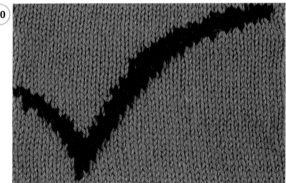

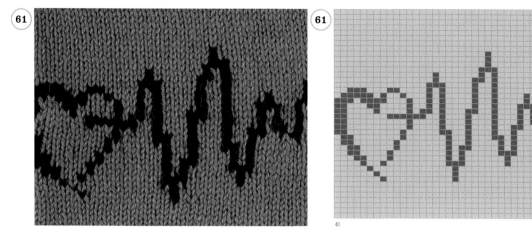

▲ *This fun chart plays on the heart and zigzag shapes made possible by playing with the classic chevron shape. It's still a chevron – honestly! Work the motif onto accessories such as tablet and cell-phone covers for a contemporary feel.*

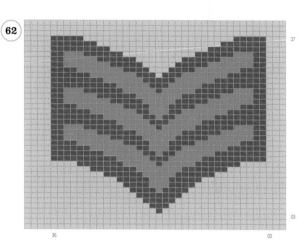

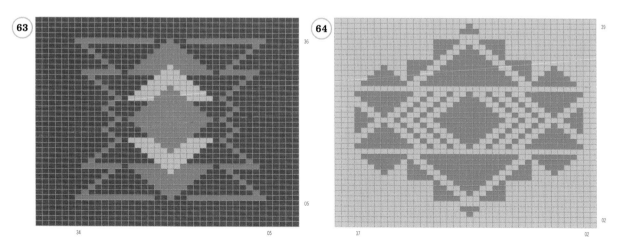

ARROWHEADS

(65)

When you break off the tip of the traditional zigzag chevron, you are left with a 'V' shape just like an arrowhead. However, not all arrowheads are equal, as you can see. Here is just a small selection of formal, abstract and optical shapes that you can add to your knitting. All are very attractive, yet they are very different in their nature.

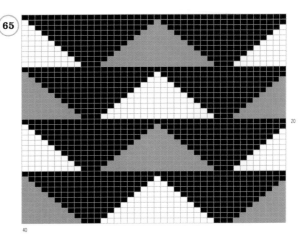

(66)

(66)

▼ *Although these two chevron charts are visually very different, both have an Art Deco feel to them. Both patterns might well have been in vogue in the 1920s – an era in which designers embraced geometric shapes and monochrome colours. Work Chart 67 using bobbins of colour (see page 236) but tackle Chart 68 differently by stranding the two colours across the back (see page 239) and carrying the yarn up the side of the work as you go.*

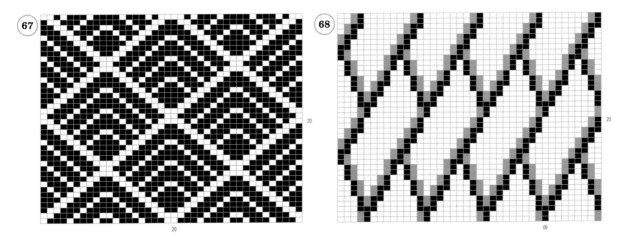

(67)

(68)

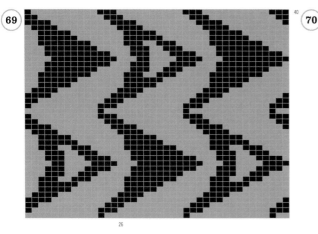

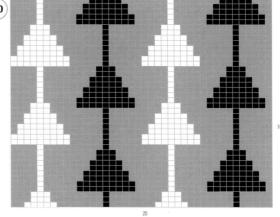

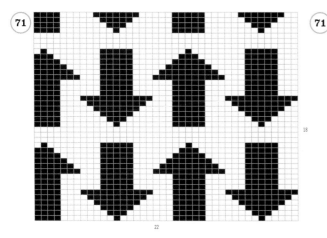

▲ Arrows are a form of the chevron and here we've taken that idea and run with it. This is a fantastic fun chart for projects and accessories. The arrows could also be used sideways as a border or singularly on clothing unless you're daring enough to cover your sweater all over and go all out for the escaped convict look!

BORDERS AND BANDS

The regularity of the chevron shape makes it an obvious choice for borders and bands. Knitted onto a cuff or hem, the classic zigzag will never date and will always add extra pizzazz to any garment.

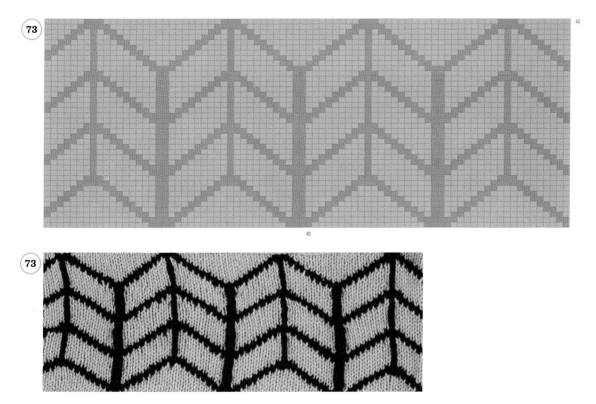

▼ *If you select this border to use along the lower edge of your project, why not add tassels at the base of every vertical stripe across the pattern? Use alternating colours or only one to add a striking accent to this chevron border.*

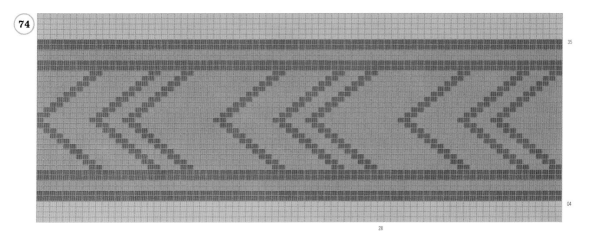

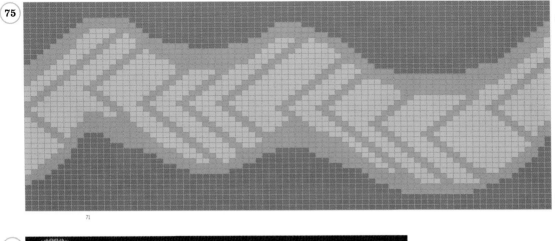

75

37

71

03

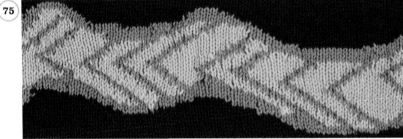

75

▲ This border is a great option for those of you who hate too much regularity in their geometry. The chevrons run sideways and point to the left of the work but the edges are wavy and run in ripples just to mix things up a little. This chart could add an interesting twist if used along the edge of a regular shaped rectangular rug, cushion cover or afghan.

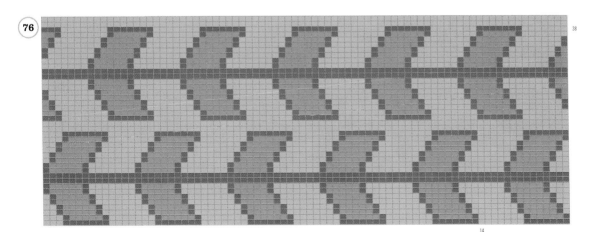

76

38

14

CHEVRON SCARF

This stitch pattern is worked over only two rows, so you will very quickly settle into the rhythm of it. We've chosen a colour palette with toning colours and a bright pop of contrast colour, but you can, of course, knit your scarf in whichever colours you love most.

YARNS

Rowan Creative Linen: 2 × 100g (219 yds) hanks in Raspberry (631) A, 1 × 100g (219 yds) hank in Leaf (632) B
Rowan Kidsilk Haze: 1 × 25g (229 yds) ball in each of Shadow (653) C, Jelly (597) D and Liqueur (595) E (C, D and E are all used double throughout)

TOOLS

Pair of 4.5mm (US 7) knitting needles
Blunt tapestry needle

TENSION

22 sts and 28 rows to 10cm (4in) using 4.5mm (US 7) needles and measured over pattern

MEASUREMENTS

23cm × 200cm (9 × 79in)

ABBREVIATIONS

See page 252

SCARF

Using yarn A, cast on 58 sts and knit 1 row.
Row 1 (RS): K1, ssk, [k10, ssk, k2tog] 3 times, k10, k2tog, k1.
Row 2: K6, [kfb of next 2 sts, k10] 3 times, kfb of next 2 sts, k6.
Rows 1–2 form the pattern and are repeated throughout.
Repeat rows 1–2, 22 times more.
Continue in pattern as set in the following stripe sequence:
14 rows in C.
[2 rows in B, 2 rows in D] 7 times.
2 rows in B.
6 rows in A.
[2 rows in C, 2 rows in E] 5 times.
2 rows in C.
46 rows in A.
Work stripe sequence 3 more times (see also chart).
Next row: Knit.
Cast off.

FINISHING

Weave in any loose ends and block according to ball band instructions.

Experiment

Why not experiment with different colour palettes for this scarf project? If you are not sure if the colours you like will work well together, try wrapping lengths of the yarns around the fat part of a ruler. Add different colours on either side and vary the width of the stripes for an instant picture of what your finished scarf will look like.

3

CHECKS AND PLAIDS

Squares and lines can be arranged in many different ways
to create patterns from simple classic checks to complex
tweedy plaids. And the process of knitting them can also
vary from simple to complex. Most patterns will require
good stranding skills (see page 239), and many will also use
the intarsia knitting technique (see page 236). However,
as always, there are ways of making many patterns
simpler to work, as some of the swatches on the
following pages will show.

PLAIDS

Plaid patterns are never out of style and can be effectively translated onto any knitting project. However, they do demand good colourwork skills if you are going to work all of them in stocking stitch. If you aren't a master knitter, then consider working parts of the patterns in texture, beading, slip stitch or embroidery; the results can be gorgeous.

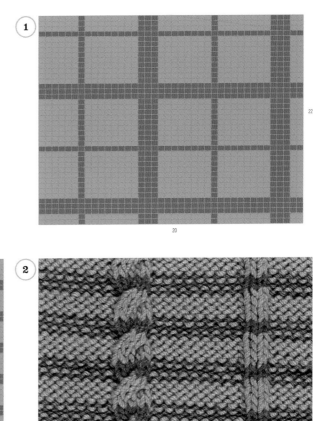

▲ Chart 2 is interpreted in a combination of texture, stitch and colour. The background is reverse stocking stitch, giving the horizontal stripes their broken edges. The verticals are created with texture, which means that the only colour knitting you are doing is simple stripes. The wider vertical stripe is a 4-stitch front cable with the twist on every sixth row, so it sits on the horizontal stripe. The narrow stripe is two stocking stitches.

5

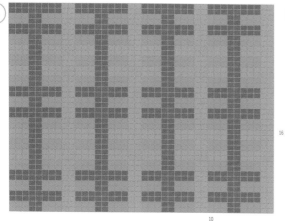

5

▲ *This slip stitch pattern changes the charted colours of the vertical stripes, but it does create an effective plaid.*

Multiple of 8 sts + 7 sts.

Row 1 (RS): Using A, knit.

Row 2: Using A, K3, k next st wrapping yarn 3 times around the needle, [k7, k next st wrapping yarn 3 times around the needle] to last 3 sts, k3.

Row 3: Using B, k3, [sl1 wyib dropping extra loops from previous row, k3] to end.

Row 4: Using B, p3, [sl1 wyif, p3] to end.

Row 5: Using C, k3, [sl1 wyib, k7] to last 4 sts, sl1 wyib, k3.

Row 6: Using C, k3, [sl1 wyif, k7] to last 4 sts, sl1 wyif, k3.

Rows 7–8: Using B, rep rows 3–4.

Row 9: Using C, knit.

Row 10: Using C, k7, [k next st wrapping yarn 3 times around the needle, k7] to end.

Rows 11–12: Using B, rep rows 3–4.

Row 13: Using A, k7, [sl1 wyib, k7] to end.

Row 14: Using A, k7, [sl1 wyif, k7] to end.

Rows 15–16: Using B, rep rows 3–4.

Rows 1–16 set pattern.

6

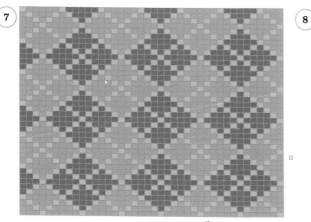

7

8

9

40

39

10

36

30

11

36

36

▼ *This pattern is perfect for stranded knitting (see page 239) as it only requires two colours, and there are never more than three stitches in a row of any colour. It's a relatively large-scale plaid, so would be perfect for a cushion cover or afghan.*

12

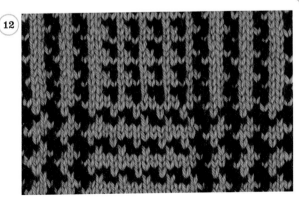

12

38

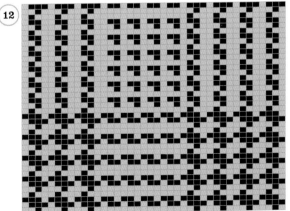

28

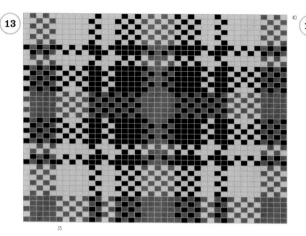

13

40

35

13

▲ This swatch is knitted in a combination of both stranded knitting (see page 239) and intarsia (see page 236), with the larger solid-colour areas being worked in the latter. This will produce a knitted fabric of different thicknesses that may not drape well if used for a loose-fitting garment.

14

40

30

15

38

30

16

40

32

DIAMONDS

The classic diamond design is the Argyle pattern, and it can be interpreted in various ways, with combinations of larger or smaller diamonds and thin or chunky lines giving different looks. As with plaids, diamond patterns often require good colour knitting skills to make the most of them.

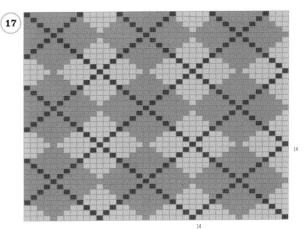

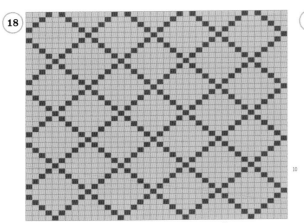

▲ *The pattern below isn't a direct translation of Chart 18 into lace (see page 247): combining colour charted patterns with texture patterns that complement them can make a project especially interesting. Self-striping yarn adds an easy colour twist.*

Multiple of 15 sts.
Row 1 (RS): [K1, p13, k1] to end.
Row 2: [P2, k11, p2] to end.
Row 3: [K3, p9, k3] to end.
Row 4: [P4, k7, p4] to end.
Row 5: [K5, p5, k5] to end.
Row 6: [K1, p5, k3, p5, k1] to end.
Row 7: [P2, k5, p1, k5, p2] to end.
Row 8: [K3, p9, k3] to end.
Row 9: As row 7.
Row 10: As row 6.
Row 11: As row 5.
Row 12: As row 4.
Row 13: As row 3.
Row 14: As row 2.
Rows 1–14 set pattern.

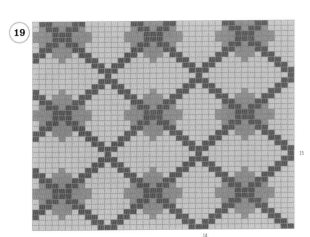

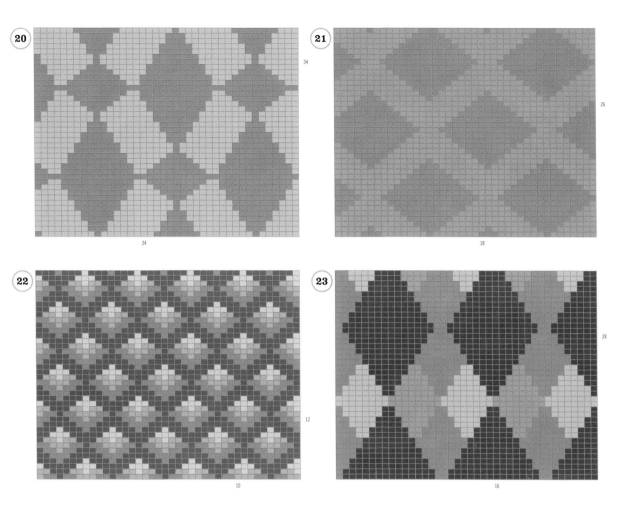

Following the chart, but using just one colour yarn to work the darker stitches in stocking stitch and the lighter ones in reverse stocking stitch, gives a textural version of the colour pattern. Always work a swatch if you're planning this approach, as patterns sometimes don't turn out as you might expect.

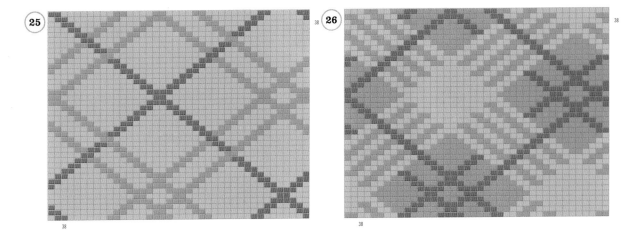

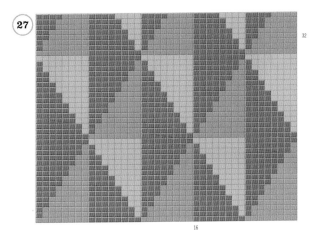

▼ You can also combine garter stitch with stocking stitch to create texture patterns from colour charts. This will work best on bold, simple patterns. But keep in mind that garter stitch has a different row height to stocking stitch, so large-scale patterns might drape oddly over a big piece of knitted fabric.

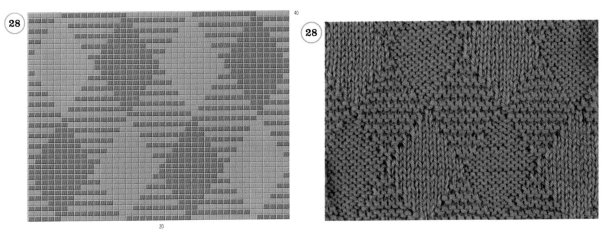

29

16

20

30

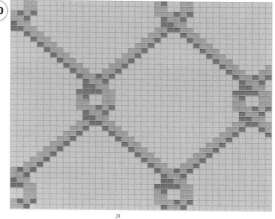

36

24

31

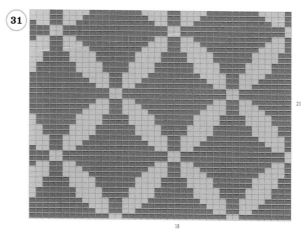

23

18

▼ *Although this doesn't look anything like a Fair Isle pattern, it is worked entirely in stranding (see page 239), for which it is perfectly suited as there are never more than two stitches between colours. If you are a novice colour knitter, then a pattern like this, which doesn't have long floats on the back, can be a good one to try.*

32

32

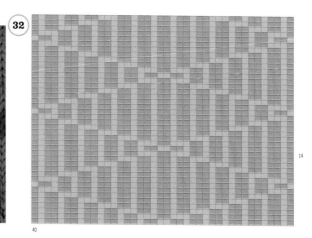

14

40

CLASSIC CHECKS

Check patterns can be perfectly simple or creatively complex, and there are versions of them in cultures all around the globe. On the following pages, there are checks in a variety of scales, making them suitable for any project from a sweetly simple child's sweater to a serious statement blanket.

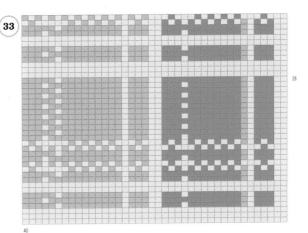

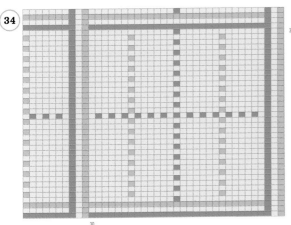

▲ Formed just from lines, this pattern lends itself perfectly to beading (see page 249). Be aware that a lot of beads will add considerable weight to a knitted fabric, changing the drape completely, and possibly stretching it out of shape over time.

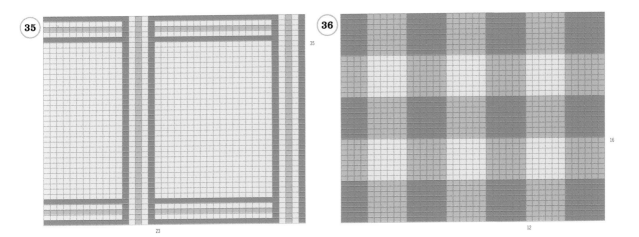

37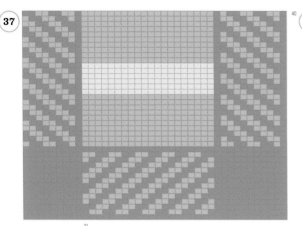

37

▲ *The large solid-colour areas are worked in intarsia (see page 236), and the cross-hatched areas in stranded knitting (see page 239). Take the time to plan out how you are going to work a pattern, from a technical point of view, before you start a project, knitting more than one swatch if need be to work out the best approach.*

38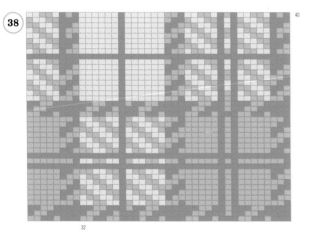

39

40

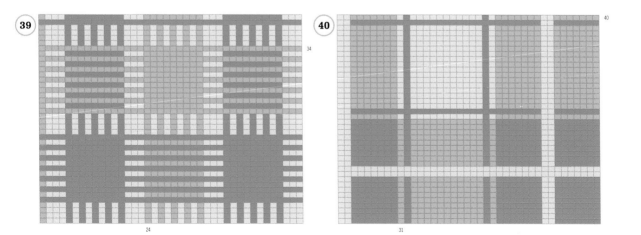

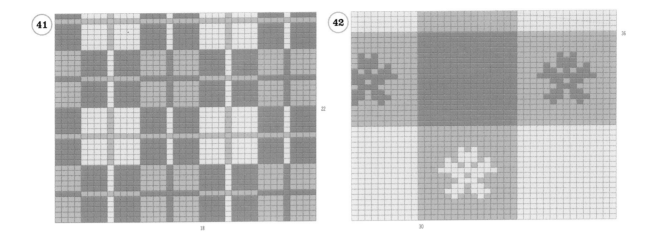

41

18 / 22

42

30 / 36

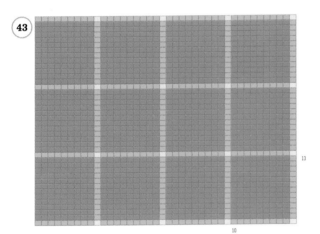

43

10 / 13

▼ This is a great example of a check pattern that looks more complicated than it is. It only uses two colours in any row, and as there are no more than four stitches between colours, you can strand it (see page 239) without having to weave in the floats (see page 241).

44

10 / 13

44

45

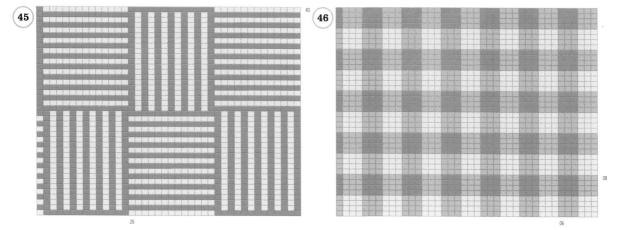

40

26

46

08

06

47

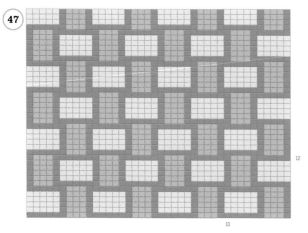

12

10

▼ *Here, the darkest colour lines are Swiss darned (see page 241).*
Do be aware that embroidery will almost always affect the drape of
knitted fabric; it will become stiffer and the embroidered sections can
hang awkwardly if they are densely stitched.

48

18

22

48

HOUNDS-TOOTH CHECKS

Although houndstooth is a very traditional design, it's been interpreted in different ways and used in the edgiest fashion designs. Black and white is the classic colour choice, but you can push the boundaries further by working the patterns in colour palettes from clashing neons to soft pastels, though working a swatch beforehand is always advisable.

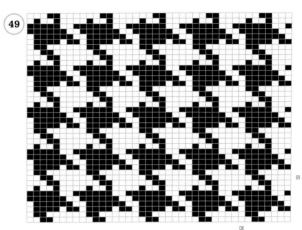

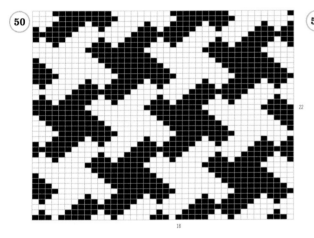

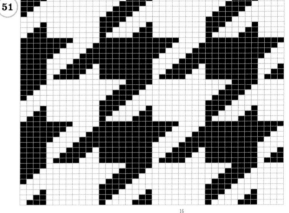

▼ *Larger-scale houndstooth patterns can be effectively worked in texture rather than colour; here, a combination of stocking stitch and garter stitch have been used. The result is relatively subtle, but very sophisticated.*

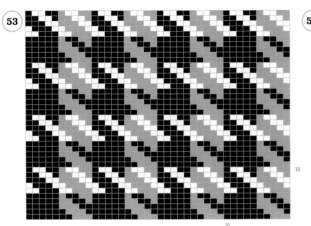

10

10

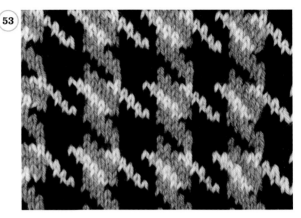

▲ This interpretation of houndstooth is uber-modern. It also requires good stranding skills (see page 239), as it uses three colours on half of the rows, and some of the floats on the back are quite long and need careful gauging.

54

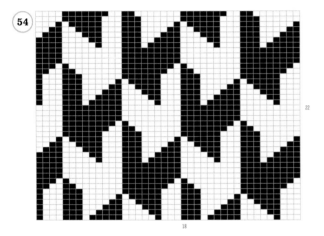

22

18

55

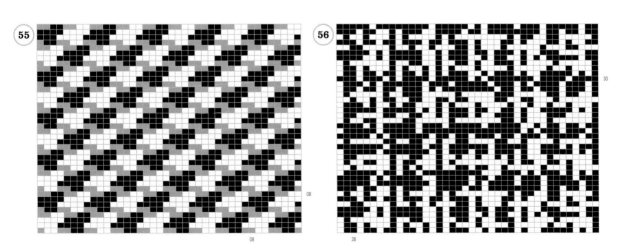

08

08

56

30

38

COMBINED CHECKS

This is the complicated end of the check spectrum. Here, checks from other pages have been combined to produce creative, unique patterns that will be a challenge to knit. You'll need to follow the charts very carefully.

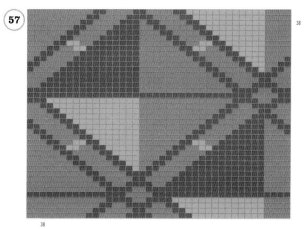

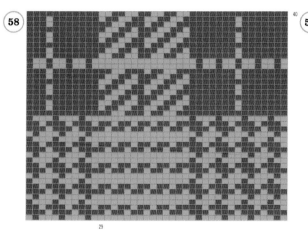

▲ *The large solid-colour areas are worked in intarsia (see page 236), and the cross-hatched areas in stranded knitting (see page 239). This will produce a knitted fabric of different thicknesses, so bear that in mind when deciding to use this pattern in a project.*

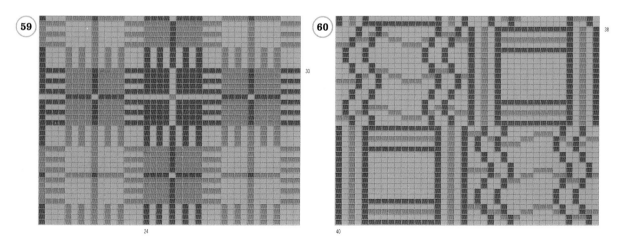

61

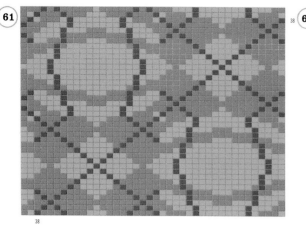

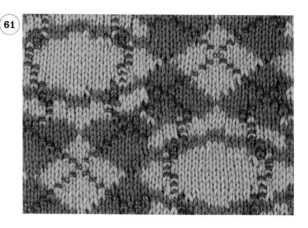

▲ *This is a very complicated design and has been pushed further by replacing all the thin dark lines with beads (see page 249). Another option would be to embroider the lines with Swiss darning (see page 241).*

62

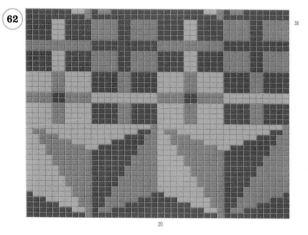

63 **64**

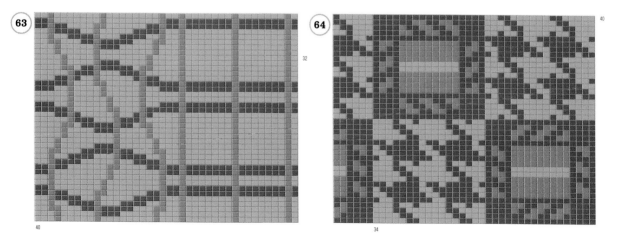

THREE-DIMENSIONAL PATTERNS

The blocky geometry of checks and diamonds lends itself well to three-dimensional patterns, but the results are hugely dependent on your colour choices. It's well worth knitting swatches in a variety of palettes to see how effective the three-dimensional aspect is before buying a lot of yarn for a project.

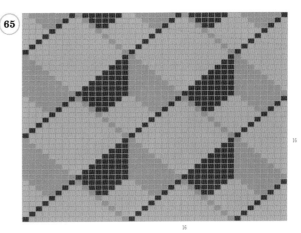

65

66

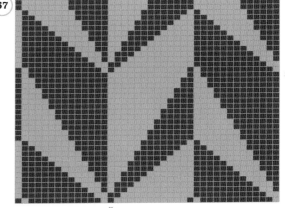

67

▼ *This is a classic pattern that needs a palette of three colours with strong contrasts to work to best effect. It also requires good intarsia knitting skills (see page 236), and there will be a lot of ends to darn in (see page 250).*

68

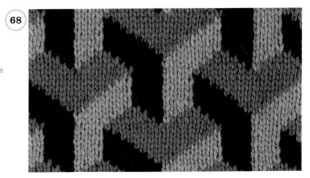

68

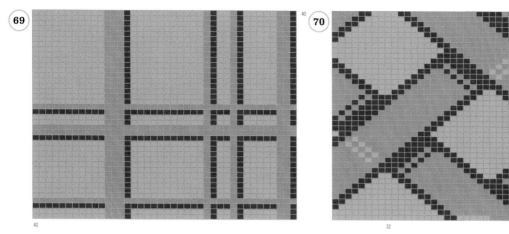

69

40

40

70

32

32

71

20

20

▼ The colour knitting aspect of this chart has been simplified by working the lines in beads (see page 249). There are a lot of beads and they will add considerable weight to a knitted fabric, changing the drape completely and stretching it out of shape over time; so this version of the pattern would be best used on a smaller project, or a cushion cover.

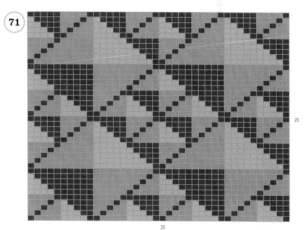

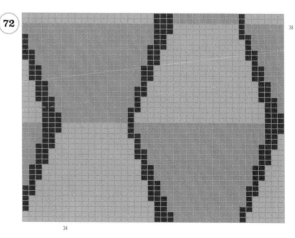

72

38

34

72

NON-STRAIGHT LINES

Checks can be curvy! Here is a selection of unique check patterns that exploit irregular lines to make the shapes, though they do all repeat so you can knit them as overall patterns on large projects. It's an interesting and fresh twist on check and plaid patterns.

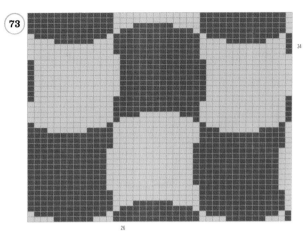

▼ *All the lines on this swatch are Swiss darned (see page 241); there's no actual colour knitting at all. Do be aware that embroidery will almost always affect the drape of knitted fabric; it will be stiffer and the embroidered sections can hang awkwardly if they are densely stitched.*

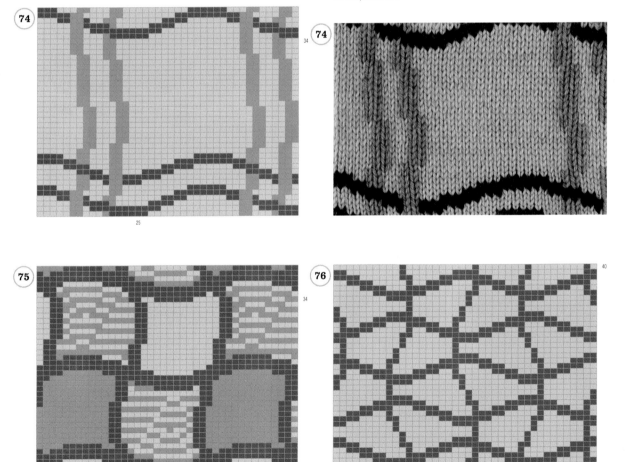

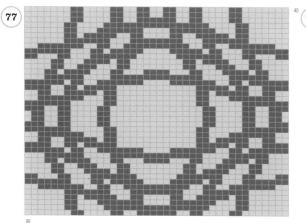

77

77

▲ *Texture knitting sometimes works surprisingly well on more complex designs, and this pattern is effectively reversible, making it a great option for an item such as a scarf. You could work most of the scarf in stocking stitch and work the ends in texture pattern for a finishing detail.*

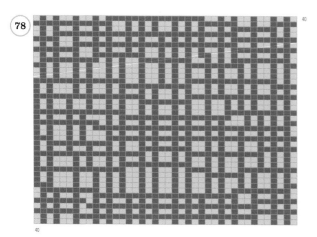

78

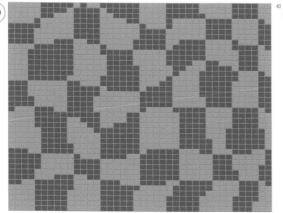

79

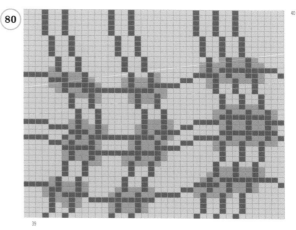

80

CHECKS AND COLOUR

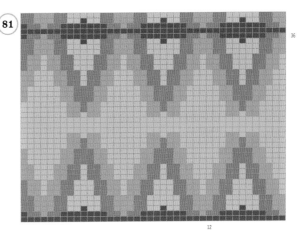

All of the patterns on this spread have appeared on other pages in this chapter, but here they are transformed by use of colour. Whether you add a tiny dash of popping colour as an accent, or throw the rainbow at a pattern, colour can entirely change and invigorate a very simple design.

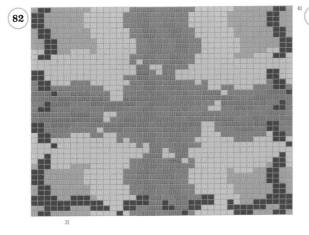

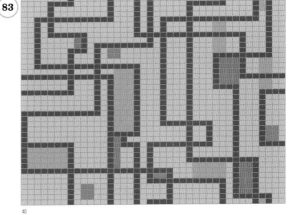

▼ This swatch is knitted using the intarsia technique (see page 236), with the horizontal dark lines worked as stripes. The vertical lines are Swiss darned (see page 241) over the intarsia joins, which makes the colour knitting easier, and has the benefit of covering any less-than-perfect stitches.

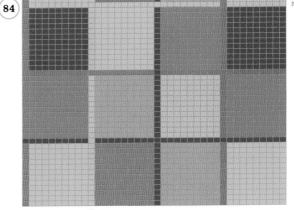

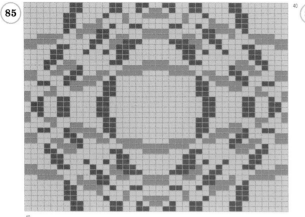

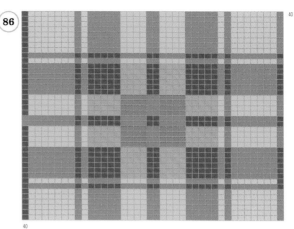

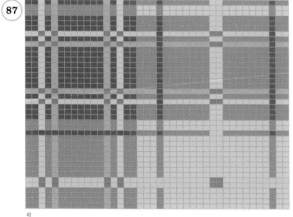

▼ *Bold, intense colour makes a serious statement, and if it feels a bit too much for an all-over pattern, try working the repeat as a border or a band within a section of plain knitting. This swatch has the solid-colour areas worked in intarsia (see page 236), and the cross-hatched areas in stranding (see page 239).*

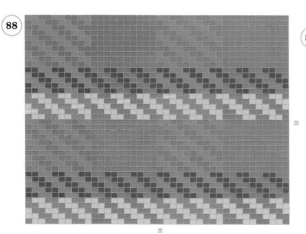

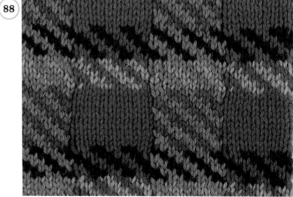

PLAID PET BED

This is a quick and easy way of creating a plaid knitted fabric, and if you think that the finished result looks too lovely to be covered in cat hair and will be much better on your sofa, we won't tell...

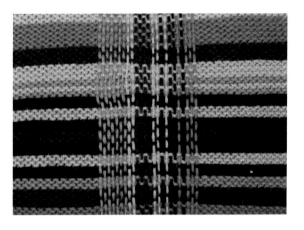

YARN
Rowan Pure Wool Worsted
1 ×100g (219 yds) ball in each of Apple (129) A, Periwinkle (146) B, Hawthorn (141) C, Almond (103) D, Damson (150) E, Grasshopper (130) F, and Ocean (145) G

TOOLS
Pair of 4mm (US 6) knitting needles
120cm (47in) 4mm (US 6) circular needle
4 stitch markers
38 × 50cm (15 × 20in) of fabric for back of pet bed
Sewing machine
Sewing thread to match fabric
38 × 38cm (15 × 15in) pad

MEASUREMENTS
38cm × 38cm (15 × 15in)

TENSION
21 sts and 40 rows to 10cm (4in) over garter stitch using 4mm (US 6) needles

ABBREVIATIONS
See page 252

PET BED
Using 4mm (US 6) knitting needles and A, cast on 65 sts. Work in garter st throughout in the following stripe sequence.

26 rows in A.
6 rows in B.
6 rows in C.
4 rows in D.
4 rows in E.
4 rows in F.
4 rows in E.
4 rows in D.
4 rows in E.
4 rows in F.
4 rows in E.
2 rows in D.
2 rows in G.
2 rows in D.
6 rows in G.
6 rows in C.
10 rows in B.
6 rows in G.
2 rows in D.
2 rows in G.
2 rows in D.
2 rows in G.
2 rows in D.
2 rows in G.
2 rows in D.
4 rows in G.
10 rows in A.
Cast off.

WOVEN SECTIONS

The plaid effect is created by weaving different-coloured yarns up and down over the garter stitch ridges. In each section, start by anchoring the yarn at the cast on edge and then weave over the bump of one ridge and under the bump of the next. Make sure that you keep the tension of the stitches quite loose to avoid pulling in the knitting.

Left-hand column

Start at the 11th st in from the left-hand side of the work and weave columns in the following sequence:

2 lines in B.

4 lines in F.

3 lines in E.

3 lines in G.

Centre column

Start at the 29th st in from the left-hand side of the work and weave columns in the following sequence:

4 lines in D.

3 lines in A.

2 lines in G.

4 lines in C.

2 lines in F.

1 lines in E.

1 lines in F.

2 lines in E.

2 lines in B.

1 lines in E.

3 lines in B.

Right-hand column

Start at the 55th st in from the left-hand side of the work and weave columns in the following sequence:

2 lines in E.

3 lines in A.

FINISHING

Weave in any loose ends and block according to ball band instructions.

Cut the piece of backing material in half across the width. Press under and sew a double 1cm ($^3/_8$in) hem at one long end of each piece. Lay the knitted piece flat and RS up. Lay one backing piece RS down on top of the knitted piece, with the hemmed end towards the middle and matching all other raw edges. Lay the second piece on top in the same way, so that the hemmed ends overlap in the middle of the knitted piece. Using straight stitch and taking a 1cm ($^3/_8$in) seam allowance, machine-sew right around the edges of the pet bed. Turn RS out and insert pad.

4

TESSELLATING AND INTERLOCKING PATTERNS

Patterns that tessellate are those in which a single repeated shape fits together, without gaps, to create an overall pattern. Interlocking patterns feature more than one shape, but the shapes fit neatly together. These patterns vary from the very simple to the very intricate, and this chapter includes some large-scale patterns that would work very well for afghans or cushions.

SIMPLE PATTERNS

On these four pages you'll find a selection of straightforward tessellating and interlocking patterns. If you are new to colour knitting, then try using the stranding technique (see page 239).

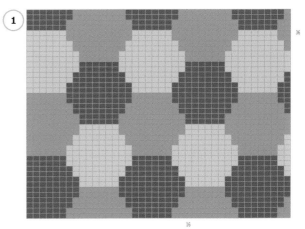

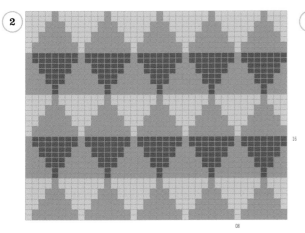

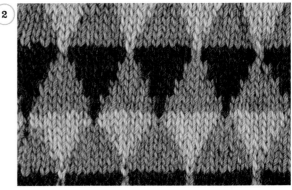

▲ *You can add a textural element to a pattern by knitting a repeat element in a fluffy yarn. Here, a fine mohair yarn is used double to make it a similar weight to the other yarns used to knit the swatch. Plying yarns up in this way will usually be effective, but you do need to knit a tension swatch to make sure that the fabric is even from section to section.*

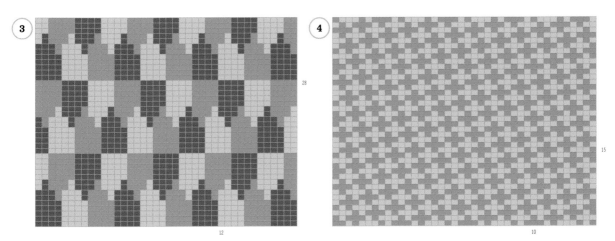

5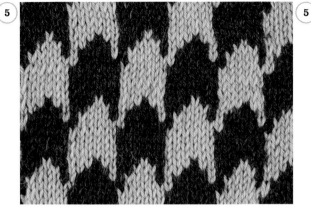

5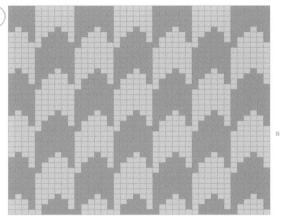

▲ This chart was knitted using the stranding technique (see page 239), but as there are six stitches between colours at some points, the floats on the back are quite long. Long floats require good colour knitting skills to get right: too tight and the fabric will pucker, too long and the edge stitches will be come baggy. If you are concerned about getting the float tension right, weave in the yarn (see page 241) on the back to make shorter floats.

6

7 **8**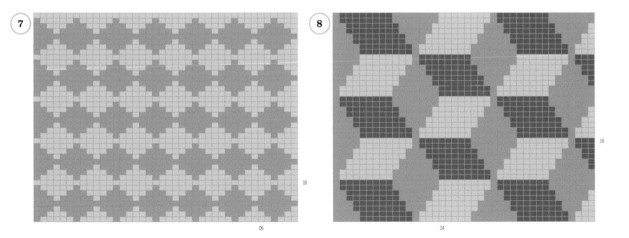

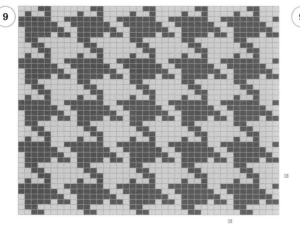

08

08

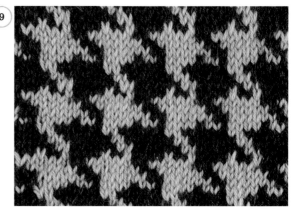

▲ *A classic houndstooth design can be given a contemporary twist by knitting it in a palette other than the traditional black and white. Here, it's two shades of green, but clashing colours can make an even bolder statement.*

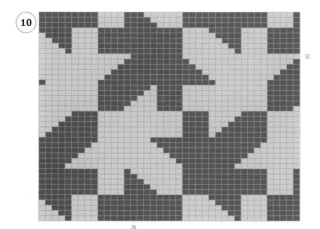

32

26

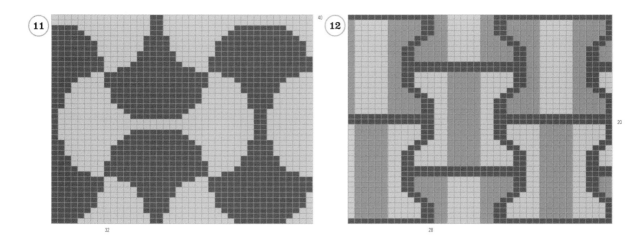

40

32

20

28

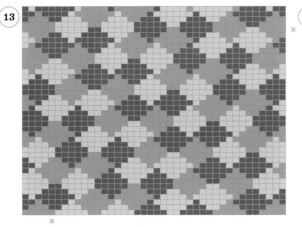

13

36

36

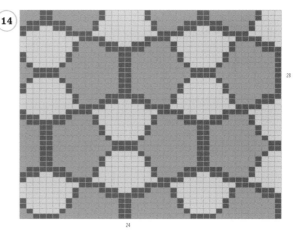

14

28

24

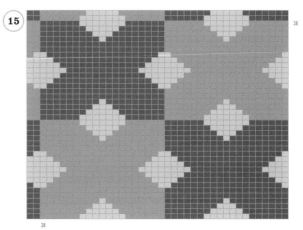

15

38

38

▼ *It can be well worth graphing out large-scale patterns if you're going to use them on an item such as a sweater. Draw out the whole pattern piece on graph paper (regular square graph paper is OK) then start by putting one pattern element in the middle, or at whatever focal point you want. You can then work out towards the edges and the pattern will be perfectly placed on the piece of knitting.*

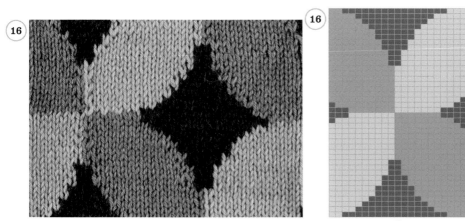

16

16

40

30

BARGELLO PATTERNS

This traditional style of canvas embroidery, sometimes called Florentine embroidery, uses tessellating shapes and stacked lines to create intricate designs that look far more complex to work than they actually are. Not all bargello patterns translate into knit – and some of those that do require impeccable colourwork skills – but here is a selection of patterns interpreted for knit and for various skill levels.

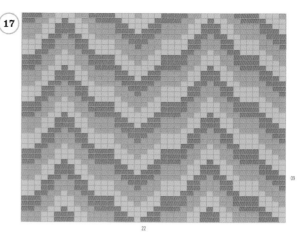

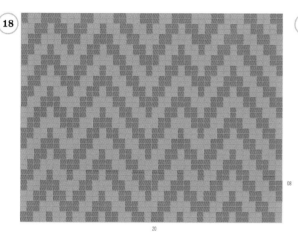

▲ The classic 'mountain peaks' bargello design is a good example of a pattern that is much easier to knit than it might look. The narrow lines are the perfect vehicle for the stranding technique (see page 239), with no weaving in required, so it's not difficult to keep the tension of both yarns even. And once the repeat is set up, the pattern is simple enough to follow easily.

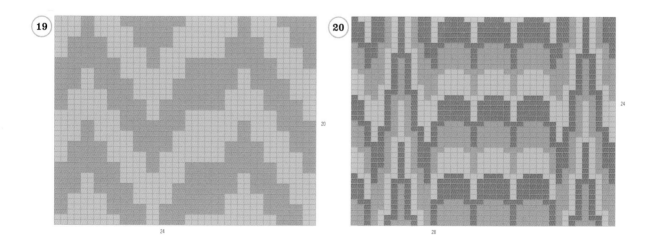

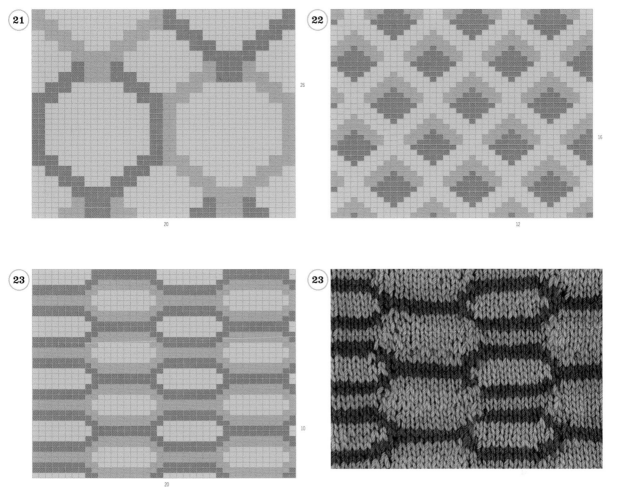

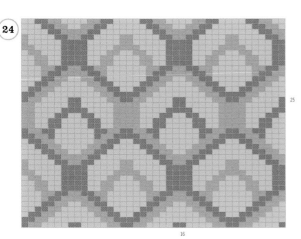

▲ *This swatch is also worked using stranding (see page 239), but be-cause yarns need to span a large number of stitches on the back of the work, they will need to be woven in (see page 250). This technique will always show a bit on the right side, with flecks of colour appearing through the stitches, so if you want one colour to be a high contrast to the others, as here, then you might prefer to Swiss darn (see page 241) some elements of the design.*

SHAPES WITH DIFFERENT CENTRES

These are more complex tessellating shapes, as the basic shapes have different central shapes. You will need to perfect your colourwork skills and follow the charts very carefully to knit these patterns; but they are beautiful so the results are worth the effort.

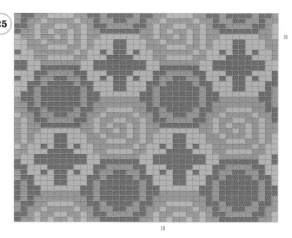

▼ This swatch has the basic shape outlines and the whole of the windmill-style centre worked in intarsia (see page 236), and the target centre and star centre are Swiss darned (see page 241). Combining techniques like this can make colour knitting less tricky to do, but do bear in mind that a lot of Swiss darning can change the drape of knitted fabric.

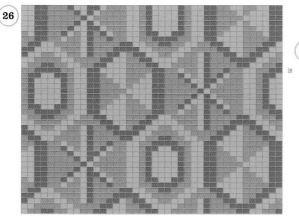

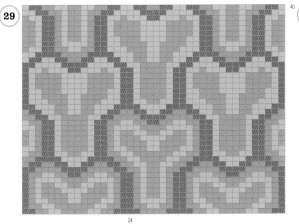

29

24

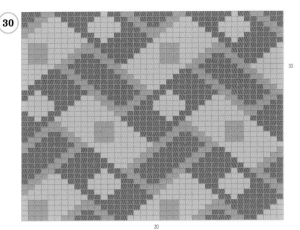

30 40

30

20

▼ Once you've mastered colour knitting, you can take it a step further by incorporating texture. You need to be aware of how colours can split across the join if there are purl stitches involved, but the effect can work positively. Always do a swatch to check you're happy with the result before embarking on a project.

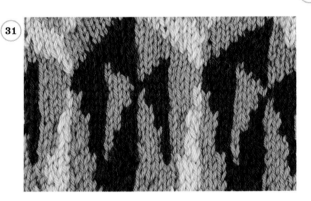

31

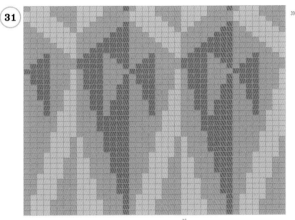

31 39

16

32 40

40

INTERLOCKING PATTERNS

On the following four pages are large-scale interlocking patterns that are perfect for big, flat items such as afghans and cushions. It's worth graphing out larger-scale patterns if you're going to use them on an item such as a sweater. Draw out the whole pattern piece on graph paper (normal square graph paper is OK) then start by putting one pattern element in the middle, or at whatever focal point you want. You can then work out towards the edges and the pattern will be perfectly placed on the piece of knitting.

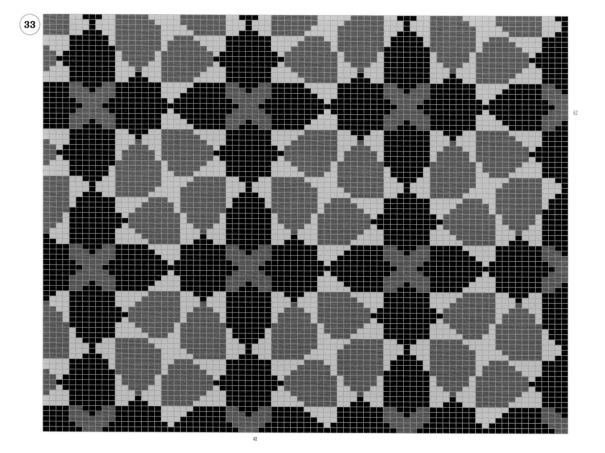

33

33

◄ *This chart was knitted using both the stranding techniques (see page 239), and the intarsia technique (see page 236). The darkest and lightest areas are intarsia knitted, with the mid-tone sections stranded in as required. This does mean that the fabric isn't an even thickness, but for an item such as a cushion, that really doesn't matter.*

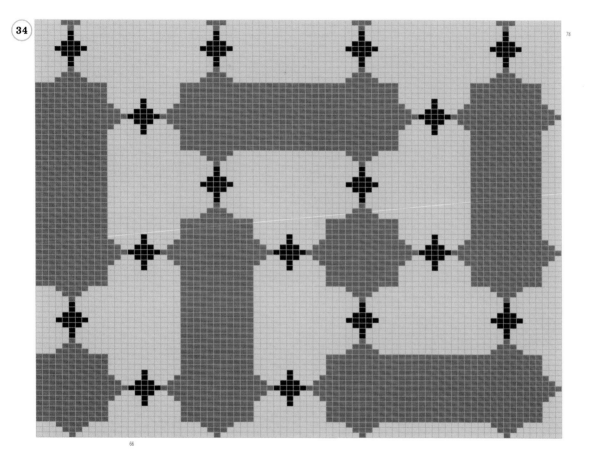

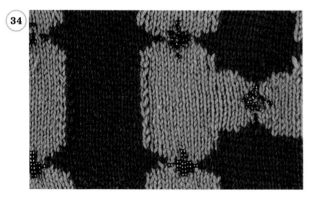

◄ *This swatch is knitted entirely in intarsia (see page 236), with the beads added to the small dark crosses (see page 249). Colour and bead knitting together does require very good colourwork skills, but you could just bead the crosses and still achieve a good effect.*

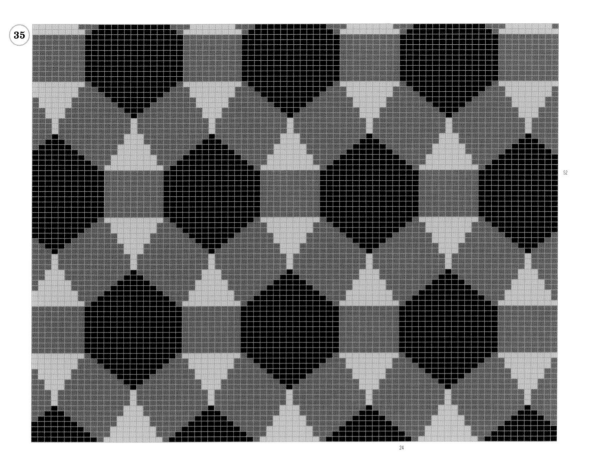

52

24

◄ *A knitter with superlative intarsia skills (see page 236) worked this swatch, as you can see by the perfect joins between colour sections. A pattern like this also leaves you with a lot of ends to darn in (see page 250) once the knitting is complete, but that does allow you to tweak stitches as you darn in and so make your colour joins beautiful.*

66

30

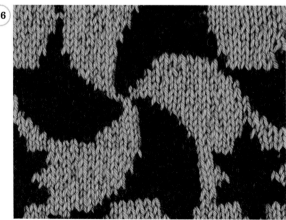

36

◄ *This swatch was stranded (see page 239), but because yarns need to span a large number of stitches on the back of the work in some places, they will need to be woven in (see page 250). This will always show a bit on the right side, with flecks of colour appearing through the stitches, but that's just inherent to the technique.*

RANDOM PATTERNS

These patterns are not truly random because they do all have a repeat; they wouldn't be very useful if they didn't! However, they look quite random, with some based on camouflage designs and others on retro prints.

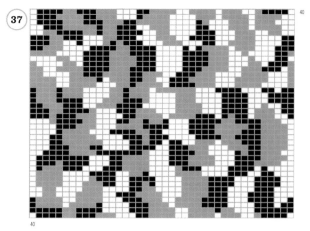

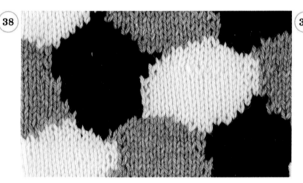

▲ *Intarsia (see page 236) is the best technique for patches of colour, though you'll have to be patient when it comes to darning in all the ends (see page 250). Tweak and ease stitches as you darn in and so make your colour joins completely perfect.*

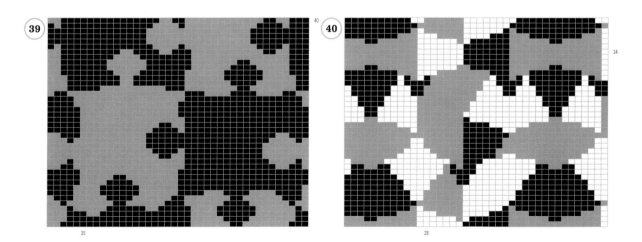

41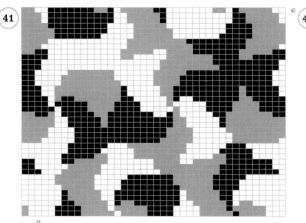

42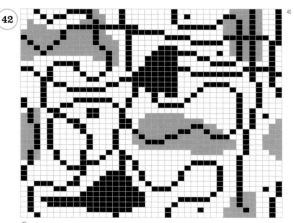

43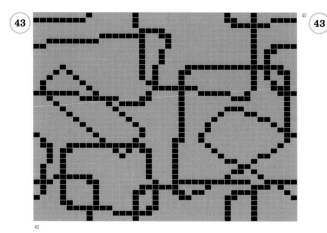

43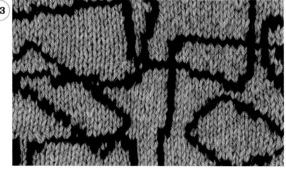

▲ *Linear patterns like this one are absolutely perfect for beading (see page 249). The technique allows you to place a bead on any stitch, so you can make the most complicated shapes. The only drawbacks are that counting and threading on the beads can take a while, and if a fabric is heavily beaded, it can pull and hang oddly.*

44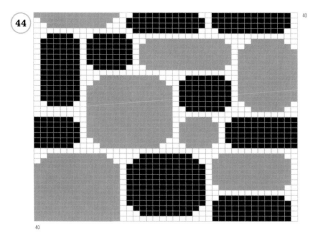

ANIMALS AND OTHERS

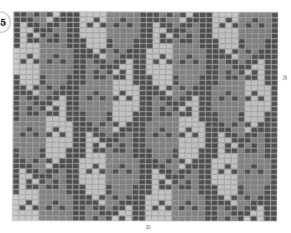

You might have to look carefully at some of the tessellating patterns to see the animals in both colours; the eye tends to pick out one colour and see the other as a background rather than a second animal. However, once you have seen them, they do look very cute!

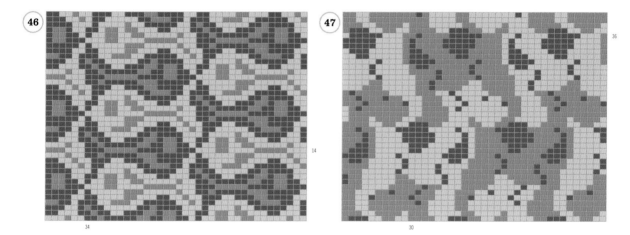

▼ *Lines and small details are often best added using Swiss darning (see page 241). For this swatch the bird shapes were intarsia knitted (see page 236), then the markings, eyes and beaks were Swiss darned. Use a yarn the same weight as the knitting yarn for the best results.*

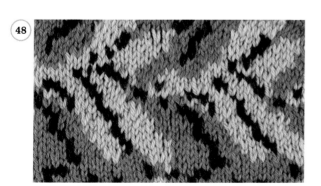

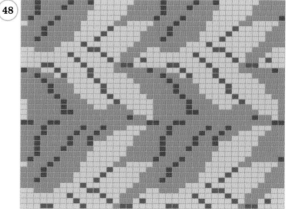

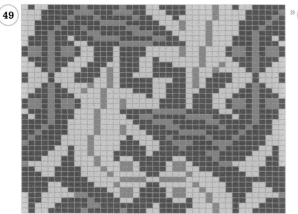

49

39

31

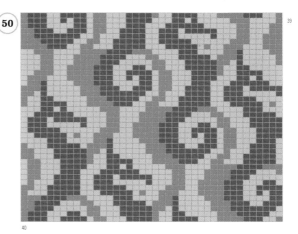

50

39

40

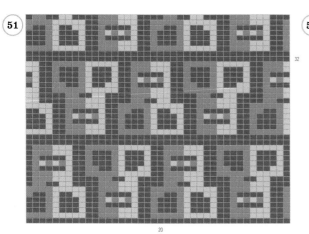

51

32

20

51

▲ *Fair Isle doesn't have to mean old-fashioned! These interlocking skulls are knitted using the stranding techniques (see page 239), and although they are a little more complex than some traditional Fair Isle patterns because they use three colours on a row rather than two, the shapes themselves are quite simple.*

52

12

16

GREEK KEY PATTERNS

These patterns are as simple and yet decorative today as they were thousands of years ago. Given here are a single motif and border patterns, as well as all-over repeats to make a full library of Greek key patterns.

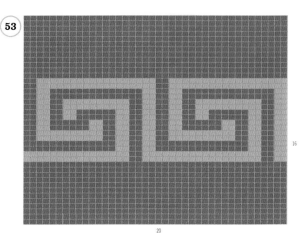

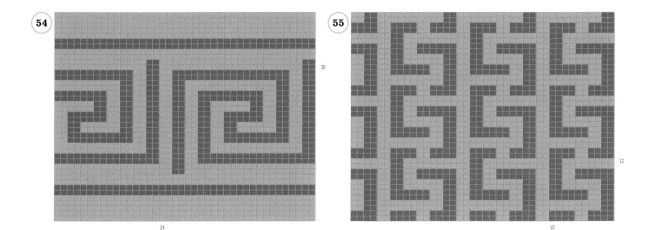

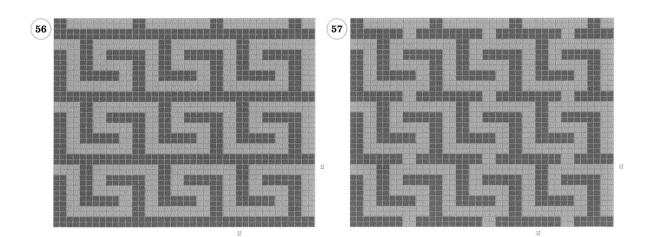

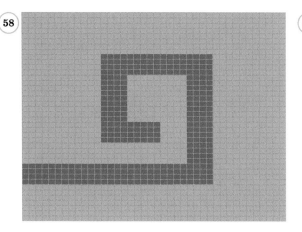

▲ *Single motifs won't affect the tension of a project and so can be worked into a plain pattern to add detail. This motif is knitted primarily using intarsia (see page 236), with the dark yarn stranded (see page 239) across the back of the inside of the key.*

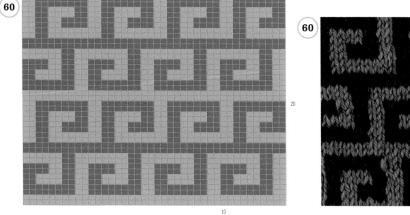

This chart can be knitted using stranding techniques (see page 239), or you can interpret it using slip stitch (see page 242), as here.

Multiple of 6 sts + 2 sts.

Rows 1–2: Using A, knit.

Row 3 (RS): Using B, k1, [sl1 wyib, k5] to last st, k1.

Row 4 and all WS rows: Work stitch sequence set in previous RS row, purling all knitted sts and slipping sts wyif.

Row 5: Using A, k2, [sl1 wyib, k3, sl1 wyib, k1] to end.

Row 7: Using B, k1, [sl1 wyib, k3, sl1 wyib, k1] to last st, k1.

Row 9: Using A, k6, [sl1 wyib, k5] to last 2 sts, sl1 wyib, k1.

Row 11: Using B, knit.

Row 13: Using A, k4, [sl1 wyib, k5] to last 4 sts, sl1 wyib, k3.

Row 15: Using B, [k3, sl1 wyib, k1, sl1 wyib] to last 2 sts, k2.

Row 17: Using A, k2, [sl1 wyib, k1, sl1 wyib, k3] to end.

Row 19: Using B, k3, [sl1 wyib, k5] to last 5 sts, sl1 wyib, k4.

Row 20: As row 4.

Rows 1–20 set pattern.

61

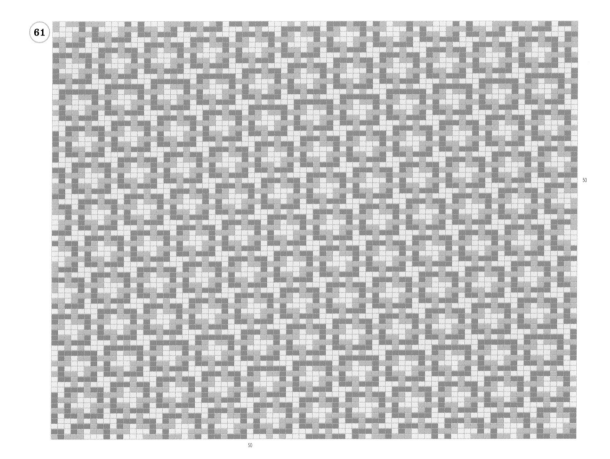

50

50

61

◀ *Although this pattern has a small-scale element, the repeat is a large one, allowing for the subtle bias-effect of the design. However, this does mean that you don't settle in to a fixed colour-change rhythm and you will have to follow the chart carefully. Knit the pattern using the stranding techniques (see page 239), which are ideal for the scale.*

62

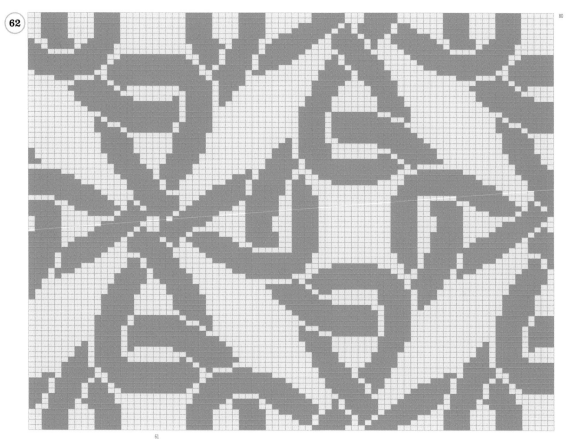

80

61

62

◀ *It can be well worth graphing out larger-scale patterns if you're going to use them on an item such as a sweater. Draw out the whole pattern piece on graph paper (normal square graph paper is OK) then start by putting one pattern element in the middle, or at whatever focal point you want. You can then work out towards the edges and the pattern will be perfectly placed on the piece of knitting.*

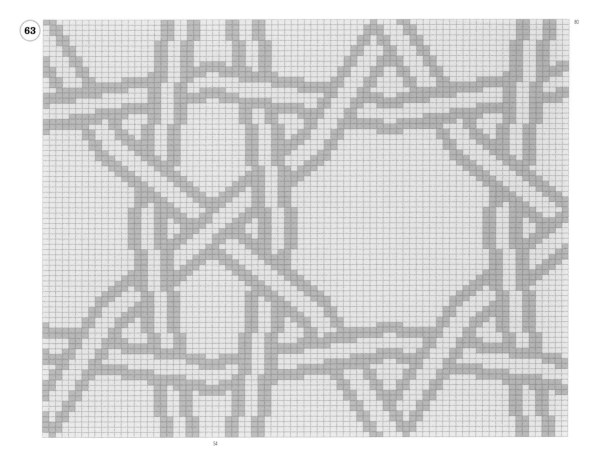

63

54

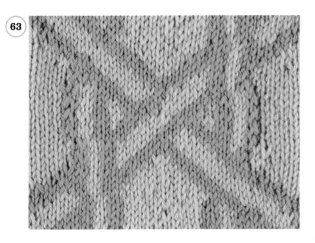

63

◀ *Patterns that consist of thin lines, like this one, can be Swiss darned (see page 241) rather than knitted if you prefer. Use a yarn that's the same weight as the knitting yarn for the best results. Bear in mind that a lot of Swiss darning can make the knitted fabric stiffer, so it won't drape in the same way as fabric that isn't embroidered.*

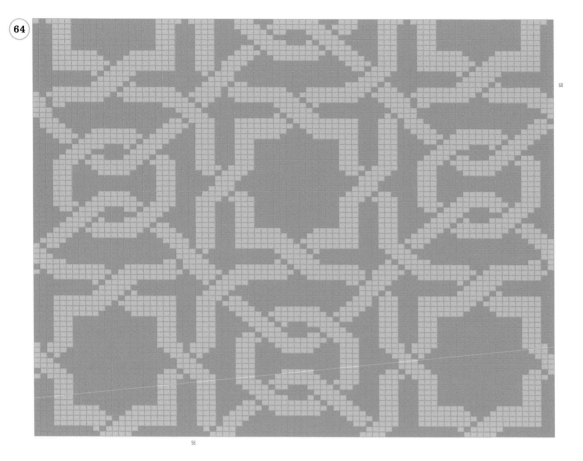

64

68

56

64

◀ *You can combine techniques very effectively to knit some patterns, though the fabric will be different thicknesses. That can be a problem if you are relying on the drape of the fabric as part of the design, but it's certainly not a problem for homewares. This swatch uses both intarsia (see page 236) and stranding (see page 239), with yarns stranded where there are only a few stitches between colours.*

HEXIE BEDSIDE MAT

As this soft, textured mat is made from tessellating hexagons, you can just keep knitting more of them and sewing them on to make a rug any size you wish.

YARNS
Rowan Pure Wool Worsted: 1 × 100g (219 yds) ball in each of Ocean (116) A, Oxygen (137) B, Grasshopper (130) C, and Moonstone (112) D

TOOLS
Pair of 4mm (US 6) knitting needles
Blunt tapestry needle
Stitch marker

TENSION
A precise tension is not essential for this pattern

MEASUREMENTS
Each hexie is 13cm (5in) across

ABBREVIATIONS
See page 252.

HEXAGON

Cast on 92 sts. Join to knit in the round, being careful not to twist stitches. Place marker to indicate beginning of round.
Knit 3 rows
Row 4 (RS): K1, [k2tog, k11, ssk] 6 times, k1. (80 sts)
Row 5: Knit.
Row 6: Knit.
Row 7: Purl.
Row 8: K1, [k2tog, k9, ssk] 6 times, k1. [68 sts]
Row 9: Knit.
Row 10: K1, [k2tog, k7, ssk] 6 times, k1. [56 sts]
Row 11: Purl.
Row 12: Knit.
Row 13: Purl.
Row 14: K1, [k2tog, k5, ssk] 6 times, k1. [44 sts]
Row 15: Knit.
Row 16: K1, [k2tog, k3, ssk] 6 times, k1. [32 sts]
Row 17: Knit.
Row 18: Knit.
Row 19: Purl.
Row 20: K1, [k2tog, k1, ssk] 6 times, k1. [20 sts[
Row 21: Purl.
Row 22: Knit.
Row 23: P1, [p3tog] 6 times, p1. [8 sts]
Cut yarn, leaving a sufficient tail to draw through rem 8 sts and pull tight and secure.
Sew side seams together using mattress st.
Work 6 hexagons in A, 6 in B, 4 in C, and 7 in D.

FINISHING

Weave in any loose ends and press according to ball band instructions.

Slip stitch hexagons together using diagram and photographs as a guide.

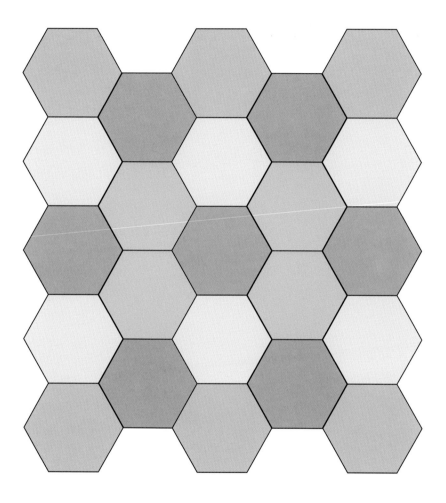

5

FROM NATURE

In this chapter we explore the geometric shapes commonly found in nature. Mother Nature's very own wonderful DNA has astounded mathematicians throughout the centuries. When looking for mathematical sequence and frequency, Fibonacci and the Golden number are found everywhere – from shell spirals to the number of petals on a flower, to the breeding patterns of honeybees. In fact, the beautiful and intricate hexagons of a honeycomb, the points of a starfish, and a spiral shell are perfect examples of how nature does things best.

FLOWERS

Although the shape and form of flowers in general vary tremendously, they do all share mathematical regularity. For instance, the number of petals in each species will always be one of the Fibonacci numbers: 3, 5, 8, 13, and so on. Combined with its obvious beauty, the geometric form of the flower makes it one of the most popular motifs found throughout knitting culture and history.

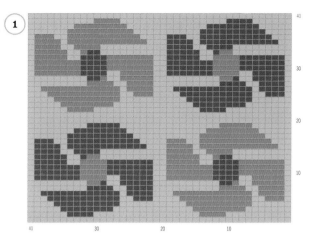

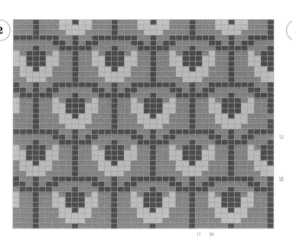

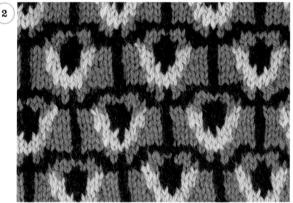

▲ I love this tulip design. Echoing the beautiful geometry of the Art Deco period, the tulips stand proud, framed in their regular boxes formed by leaf and stem. Some beads (see page 249) would add extra glamour to the centre of the tulips if you are looking for a bit of sparkle.

5

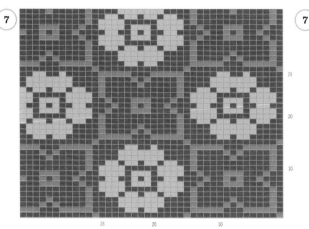

06

06

6

14

10

40

14

10

7

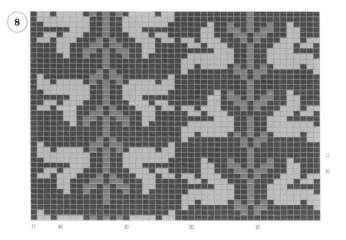

28

20

10

28

20

10

7

▲ This swatch features one of the most commonly used floral motifs. The rose shape is often used in Norwegian and Estonian folk knitting and it is also very reminiscent of the British Tudor Rose. Use small bobbins of different colours to work each flower (see page 236).

8

13

10

44   40   30   20   10

9

9

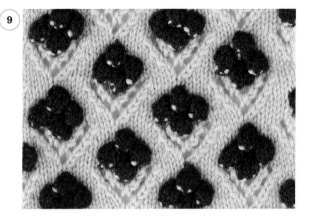

10

11

Key

⁄	RS: k2tog WS:p2tog
○	yo
＼	RS: ssk WS: p2tog tbl
◉	bobble
•	RS: purl WS: knit
□	RS: Knit WS: Purl

Row 1 (RS): [(Yo, ssk) twice, k7, (k2tog, yo) twice, k1] twice, [yo, ssk] twice, k4. [40 sts]

Row 2 and all WS rows: Purl.

Row 3: [K6, k2tog, yo, k7, MB] twice, k6, k2tog, yo.

Row 5: K1, [MB, k3, k2tog, yo, k1, yo, ssk, k3, MB, k3] twice, MB, k3, k2tog, yo, k1.

Row 7: [K4, (k2tog, yo) twice, k1, yo, ssk, k4, MB] twice, k4, [k2tog, yo] twice.

Row 9: K3, [(k2tog, yo) twice, k1, (yo, ssk) twice, k7] twice, [k2tog, yo] twice, k1.

Row 11: [K7, MB, k6, k2tog, yo] twice, k7, MB.

Row 13: [Yo, ssk, (k3, MB) twice, k3, k2tog, yo, k] twice, yo, ssk, k3, MB, k2.

Row 15: [K1, yo, ssk, k4, MB, k4, (k2tog, yo) twice] twice, k1, yo, ssk, k4, MB.

Row 16: Purl.

These 16 rows form the pattern.

▲ This pretty thistle design can be spiced up in two ways. If you'd rather not purl the centre stitches of each flower bud, why not add beads to give added interest? Use small bobbins (see page 236) to save long floats across the back of your work.

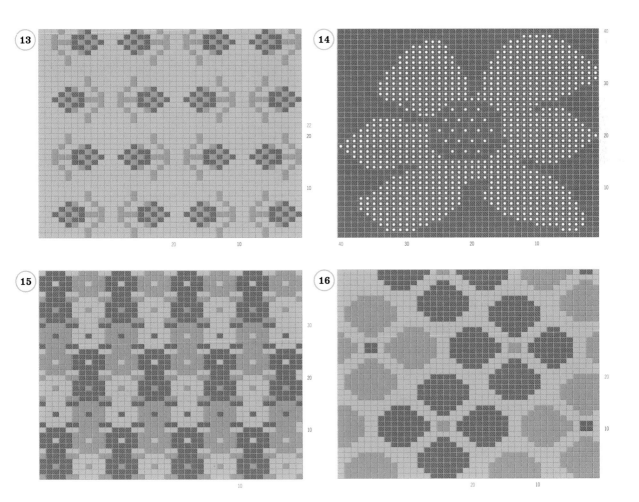

LEAVES

The humble leaf is a real thing of beauty. With skeleton veins that grow only more beautiful as the leaf dries to the abundance of spring greens, rich browns, fall reds and golds – this section celebrates leaf shapes, colours and forms in all their variety.

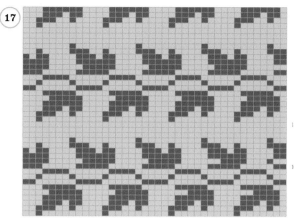

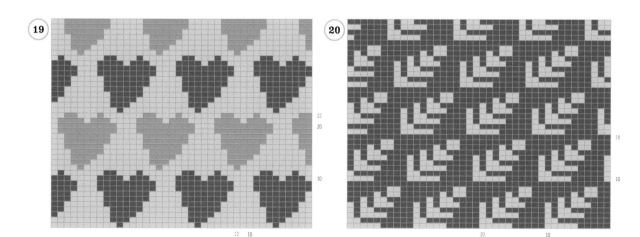

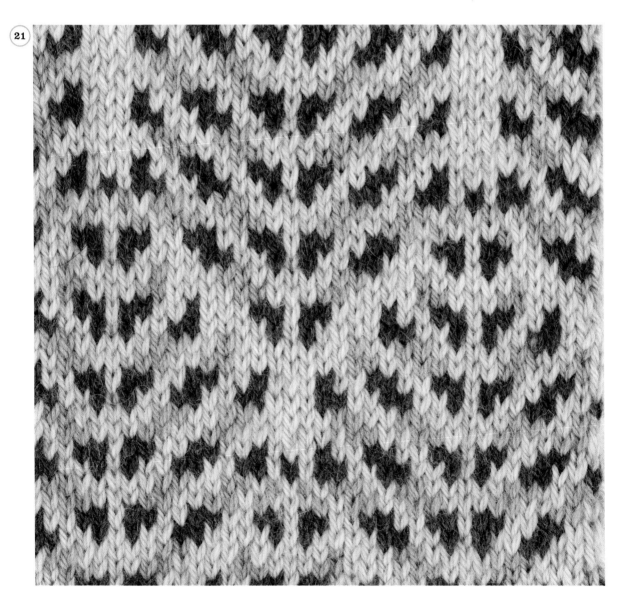

21

39

30

20

10

22 20   10

▼ *This Fair Isle leaf pattern is quick and easy to knit up. There are only two colours in use in any row at any time, so stranding is your best option for this swatch (see page 239). Try alternating light and dark colours to experiment with colour dominance. You could even use a metallic thread to add a touch of sparkle to the leaf veins.*

21

Key

- **•** RS: purl WS: knit
- **ℛ** RS: k tbl WS: p tbl
- **╱** RS: k2tog WS: p2tog
- **○** yo
- **╲** RS: sl1, K1, psso WS: p2tog tbl
- **□** RS: Knit WS: Purl

Row 1 (RS): P6, (k1 tbl, p16) twice. (40 sts)

Row 2 (WS): (K16, p tbl) twice, k6.

Row 3: P5, k1, k1 tbl, p15, k1, k1 tbl, k1, p14, k1.

Row 4: (P, k15, p tbl) twice, p1, k5.

Row 5: P4, (k2tog, yo, k1 tbl, p14) twice, k2tog, yo.

Row 6: (P2, k14, p tbl) twice, p2, k4.

Row 7: P3, (k2tog, yo, k1, k1 tbl, p13) twice, k2tog, yo, k1.

Row 8: (P3, k13, p1 tbl) twice, p3, k3.

Row 9: P2, (k2tog, yo, k2, k1 tbl, p12) twice, k2tog, yo, k2.

Row 10: (P4, k12, p1 tbl) twice, p4, k2.

Row 11: P1, (k2tog, yo, k1, k2tog, yo, k1 tbl, p11) twice, k2tog, yo, k, k2tog, yo.

Row 12: (P5, k11, p1 tbl) twice, p5, k1.

Row 13: ((K2tog, yo, k1) twice, k1 tbl, p10) twice, (k2tog, yo, k1) twice.

Row 14: (P6, k10, p1 tbl) twice, p6.

Row 15: (K2, k2tog, yo, k2, k1 tbl, k1, p9) twice, k2, k2tog, yo, k2.

Row 16: (P6, k9, p, p tbl) twice, p6.

Row 17: (K1, k2tog, yo) twice, k1 tbl, yo, sl1, k1, psso, p8) twice, (k1, k2tog, yo) twice.

Row 18: (K1, p5, k8, p2, p1 tbl) twice, k1, p5.

Row 19: (K2tog, yo, k1, k2tog, yo, p1, k1 tbl, k1, yo, sl1, k1, psso, p7) twice, k2tog, yo, k1, k2tog, yo, p1.

Row 20: (K2, p4, k7, p3, p1 tbl) twice, k2, p4.

Row 21: (K2, k2tog, yo, p2, k1 tbl, k2, yo, sl1, k1, psso, p6) twice, k2, k2tog, yo, p2.

Row 22: (K3, p3, k6, p4, p1 tbl) twice, k3, p3.

Row 23: (K1, k2tog, yo, p3, k1 tbl, yo, sl1, k1, psso, k1, yo, sl1, k1, psso, p5) twice, k1, k2tog, yo, p3.

Row 24: (K4, p2, k5, p5, p1 tbl) twice, k4, p2.

Row 25: (K2tog, yo, p4, k1 tbl, (k1, yo, sl1, k1, psso) twice, p4) twice, k2tog, yo, p4.

Row 26: (K5, p, k4, p6, p tbl) twice, k5, p1.

Row 27: P6, (k1 tbl, k2, yo, sl1, k1, psso, k2, p10) twice.

Row 28: (K10, p6, p1 tbl) twice, k6.

Row 29: P6, (k1 tbl, (yo, sl1, k1, psso, k1) twice, p10) twice.

Row 30: (K10, p5, k1, p1 tbl) twice, k6.

Row 31: P6, (k1 tbl, p1, yo, sl1, k1, psso, k1, yo, sl1, k1, psso, p10) twice.

Row 32: (K10, p4, k2, p1 tbl) twice, k6.

Row 33: P6, (k1 tbl, p2, yo, sl1, k1, psso, k2, p10) twice.

Row 34: (K10, p3, k3, p1 tbl) twice, k6.

Row 35: P6, (k1 tbl, p3, yo, sl1, k1, psso, k1, p10) twice.

Row 36: (K10, p2, k4, p1 tbl) twice, k6.

Row 37: P6, (k1 tbl, p4, yo, sl1, k1, psso, p10) twice.

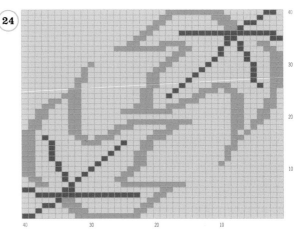

Row 38: (K10, p1, k5, p1 tbl) twice, k6.

Row 39: Repeat row 1.

Row 40: Repeat row 2.

25

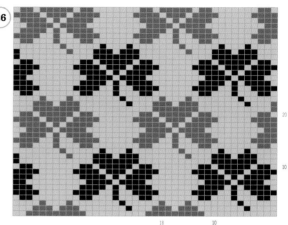

26

27

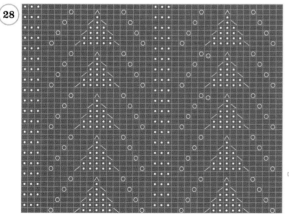

28

Key

- ⊡ b
- ◿ RS: sl1, K1, psso WS: p2tog tbl
- ◹ RS: k2tog WS: p2tog
- ⊙ yo
- ◿ RS: sl1, k2tog, psso WS:sl1 wyif, p2tog tbl, psso
- ☐ RS: Knit WS: Purl

Row 1 (RS): K1, yo, k3, sl1, k1, skpo, p5, k2tog, k3, yo, k5, yo, k3, sl1, k1, skpo, p5, k2tog, k3, yo, k4. [40 sts]

Row 2 (WS): [K3, p6, k5, p6] twice.

Row 3: K2, yo, k3, sl1, k1, skpo, p3, k2tog, k3, yo, k7, yo, k3, sl1, k1, skpo, p3, k2tog, k3, yo, k5.

Row 4: [K3, p7] 4 times.

Row 5: K3, yo, k3, sl1, k1, skpo, p1, k2tog, k3, yo, k9, yo, k3, sl1, k1, skpo, p, k2tog, k3, yo, k6.

Row 6: [K3, p8, k, p8] twice.

Row 7: K4, yo, k3, sl1, k2tog, sk2po, k3, yo, k11, yo, k3, sl1, k2tog, sk2po, k3, yo, k7.

Row 8: [K3, p17] twice.

Rows 9–40: Rep rows 1–8.

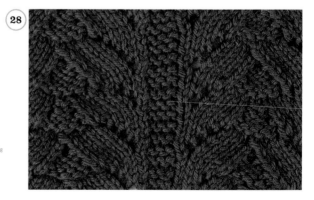

28

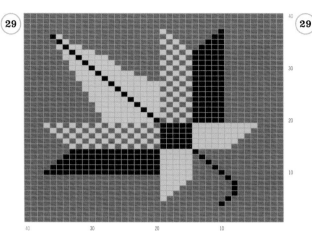

▲ *For this design, I was inspired by the geometry of quilting. I took the wonderful form of the maple leaf and divided it into blocks of colour and pattern. Use bobbins to work this swatch (see page 236). Combined with textured squares, this could make a wonderful afghan or throw.*

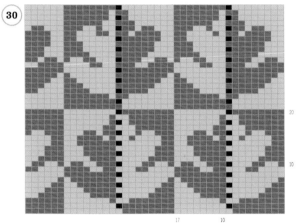

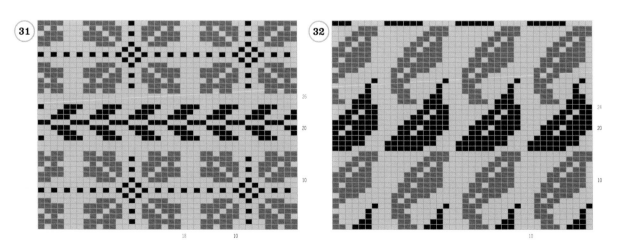

SHELLS

If you've ever collected shells from the beach you will have noticed perfect spirals, fan shapes, curves and spines. The geometry of the spiral alone is breathtaking.

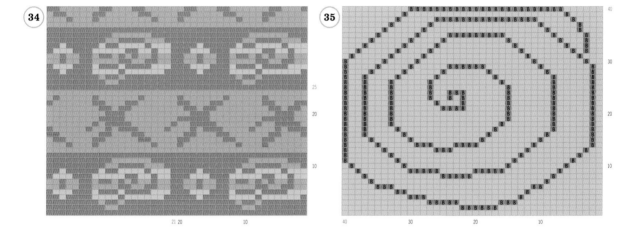

▼ These clams fit together in a geometric order much loved by the Art Deco period. Use separate bobbins of colour to work each clam.

37

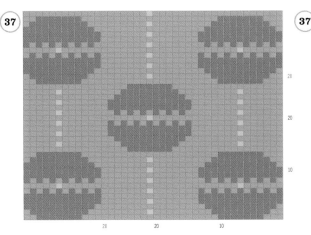

37

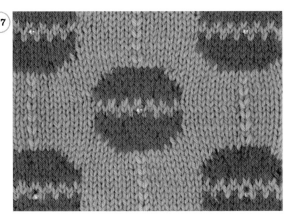

▲ *These oyster shells hold a pearl in their jaws. I've added a bead (see page 249) to each centre to add an extra dimension. If you don't like working with too many bobbins of colour, just Swiss darn (see page 241) the horizontal lines in afterwards.*

38

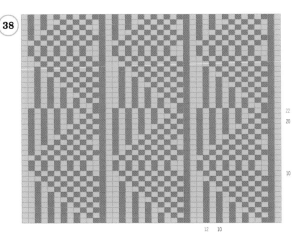

39

40

ANIMALS

I've had fun experimenting with the geometry of animals in this section. With the whole of the animal kingdom to choose from, it was hard narrowing things down to only eight. I hope you enjoy adding your own flourish to these geometric critters.

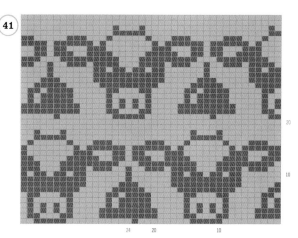

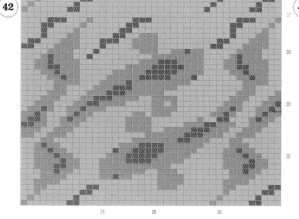

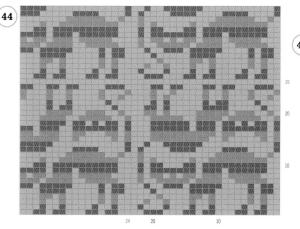

▼ These cats have their hackles raised, which makes them fit together beautifully for the purposes of this pattern. I've used alternating stripes, which means you'll only ever use two colours in any one row. Stranding (see page 239) is the best method for knitting this swatch.

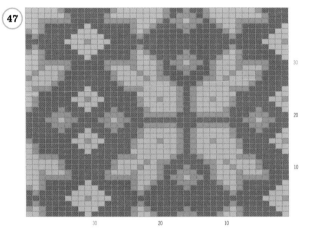

▼ *I have taken inspiration from the Aztecs for this design. These negative and positive images of a distinctly geometric dog are best knitted using bobbins of colour (see page 236).*

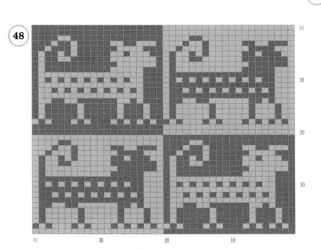

FRUIT

Who knew how much geometry was present in fruit? You'll never look at an orange segment or a bunch of grapes in the same way after you have knitted your way through my fruity selection of geometric knitting charts.

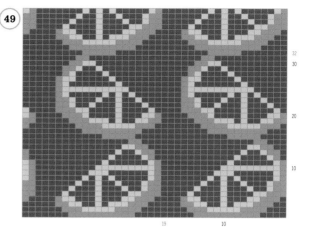

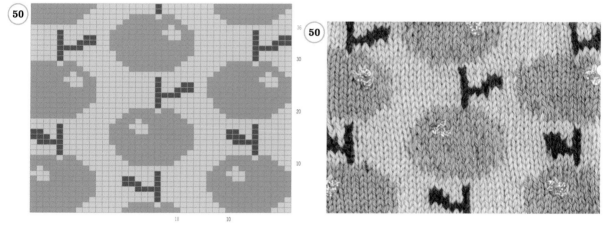

▼ *Shiny apples in a row. I've added a sequin to the apple highlights to give this swatch a bit more sparkle. Just use some matching thread and a sewing needle to sew them firmly in place.*

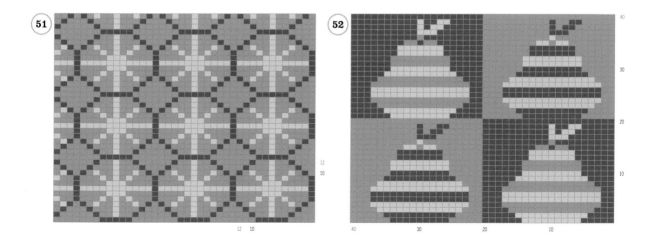

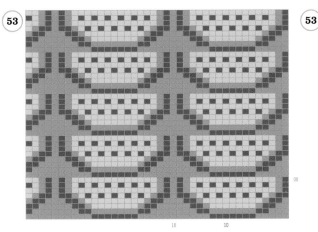

53

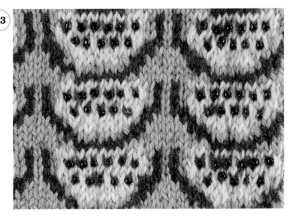

53

▲ *These juicy watermelons can be made even more mouth-watering with the addition of beads for seeds (see page 249) to bring these wedges to life.*

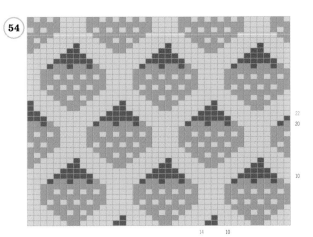

54

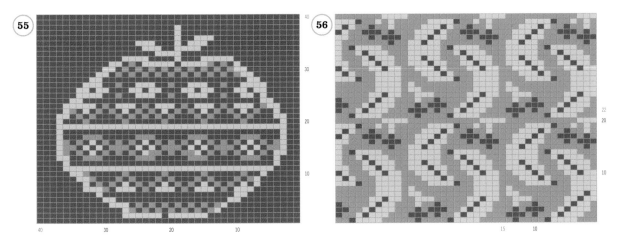

55

56

BIRDS

Birds are some of the best loved and prettiest members of the animal kingdom. There are widely differing shapes and sizes within the species: here, I have tried to explore both large and small, fliers and nonfliers, so you can choose your favourite.

▼ *This geometric hen definitely has its roots in folk art. Using only two colours per row, stranding (see page 239) is best here. Why not add some beads (see page 249) or even embroidery (see page 249) to personalise your bird?*

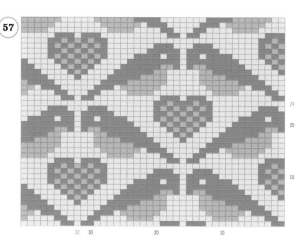

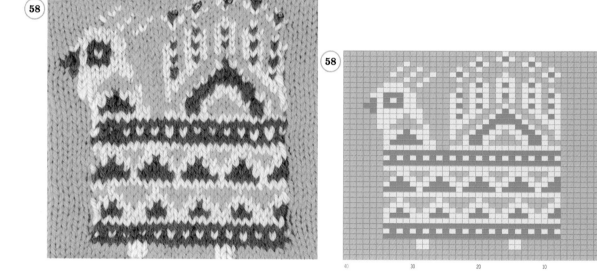

▼ *The arrow shapes of flying geese fit perfectly together here and form an attractive geometric pattern.*

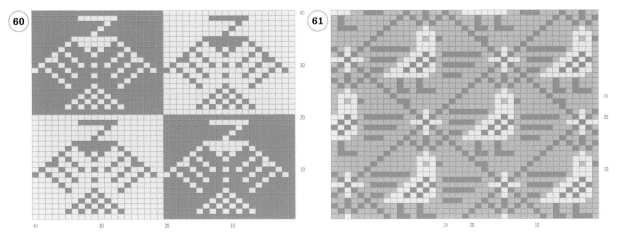

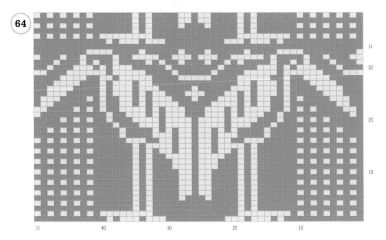

PEOPLE

Many knitters are familiar with the common Scandinavian 'paper dolls' figurative motifs. In this section, I have expanded the repertoire and taken inspiration from both folk art and fine art to design this collection of charts featuring people.

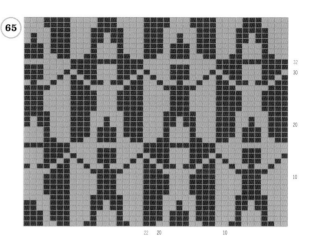

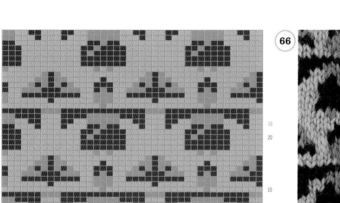

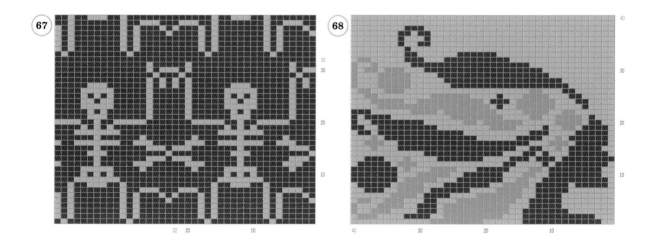

▲ I've taken inspiration from Scandinavian folk art and added an Asian twist. These geishas are holding hands in an orderly row with their fans nearby, just in case.

69

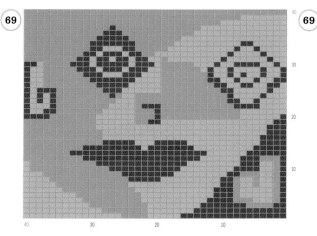

69

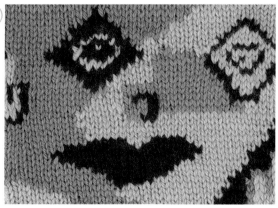

▲ *Picasso turned the human face literally on its head with his Weeping Woman painting. Here I've used geometry to design an abstract version of my own. Use bobbins of colour to work this design (see page 236).*

70

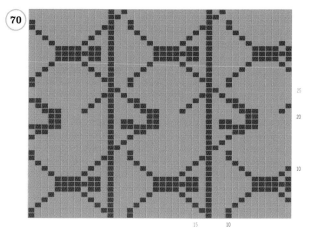

71

72

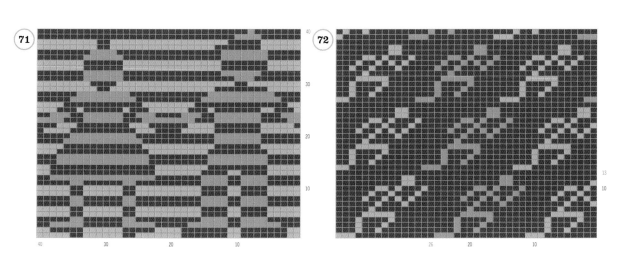

BORDERS

I've taken elements of each section to create a variety of borders with natural designs. Choose one that delights you and add it to an accessory or garment to make it your own.

▼ *Make this swatch easily by knitting the background first and then adding the leaves and stems using Swiss darning (see page 241).*

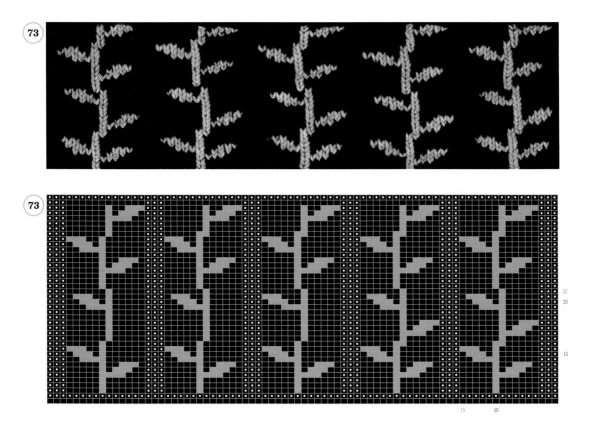

▼ *I've used leaves to form touching circles in this design. Why not add beads to the centre of the leaves to give an extra dimension (see page 249)?*

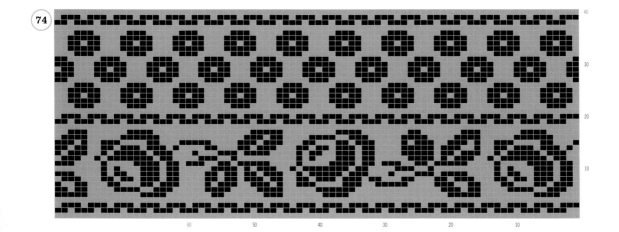

75

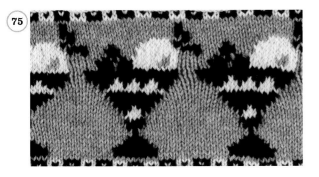

75

▲ *Bowls overflowing with fruit. You could almost be at a Roman feast in this design. Strand the yarns across the border but use bobbins of yarn for the bowls and fruit (see pages 239 and 236).*

▼ *This border has a joyous feel. The tribesmen are having a great time dancing to the beat of the drums. Add some sequins, beads or embroidery for extra sparkle and pop.*

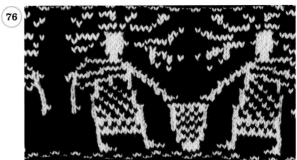

76

76

FALLING LEAVES CUSHION

This pillow has a really autumnal feel and is a great project for those new to intarsia. I have backstitched additional detail on top of each leaf, but you could also add bugle beads or leave them blank.

MATERIALS
Rowan Felted Tweed
1 × 50g (191 yds) balls each in shades Clay (A), pine (B), avocado (C), gilt (D), ginger (E), rage (F)
4mm (US 6) needles
Tapestry needle for embroidery
Sewing machine and machine sewing thread
Contrast material for cushion back approx.
30 × 43cm (12 × 17in)
Cushion pad 30cm × 30cm (12 × 12in)

TENSION
22 sts × 30 rows over 10cm (4in) using 4mm (US 6) needles and stocking stitch

MEASUREMENTS
30cm × 30cm (12 × 12in)

PATTERN
Using yarn A, CO 72 sts and beg working from the chart. Wind separate bobbins of yarn and use the intarsia method of knitting the pattern. Details of how to work intarsia can be found on page 236. When you have finished working all 80 rows of the chart, cast off kwise using yarn A.

FINISHING
Weave in any loose ends and block according to ball band instructions.

CUSHION
Using the photo as a guide, embroider veins across the leaves using a tapestry needle, contrast yarn and back-stitch. Cut the piece of backing material in half across the width. Press under and sew a double 1cm (³/₈in) hem at one long end of each piece. Lay the knitted piece flat and RS up. Lay one backing piece RS down on top of the knitted piece, with the hemmed end towards the middle and matching all other raw edges. Lay the second piece on top in the same way, so that the hemmed ends overlap in the middle of the knitted piece. Using straight stitch and taking a 1cm (³/₈in) seam allowance, machine-sew right around the edges of the cushion. Turn RS out and insert pad.

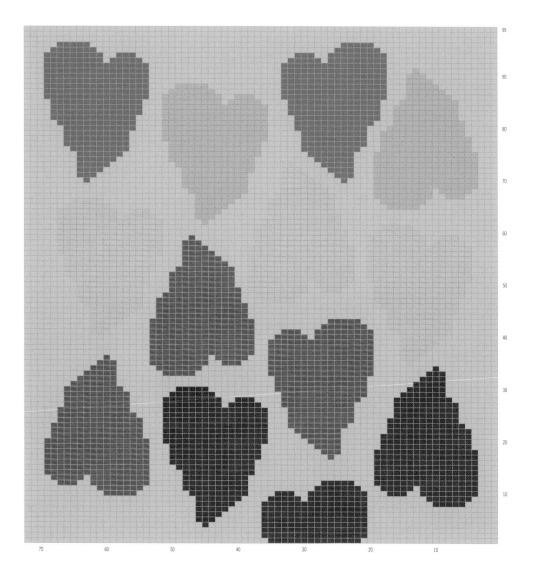

Key

- clay 177 A
- pine 158 B
- avocado 161 C
- gilt 160 D
- ginger 154 E
- rage 150 F

MOTIFS

In this chapter, we are looking at individual geometric motifs. I will explore well-known shapes such as squares, triangles, diamonds and circles before moving on to other more interesting geometrics like starbursts and hearts. In addition, I include a few geometric motifs that are familiar to Asian, Celtic and Scandinavian cultures.

CELTIC

Never-ending knots, circles, crosses and spirals are all found commonly within Celtic history and folklore. Each symbol represents an idea rooted in centuries of oral tradition and folklore. I have tried to cover the most widely used symbols here.

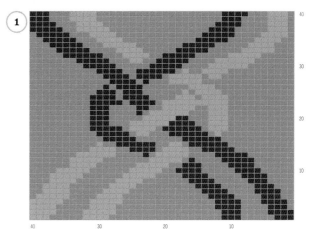

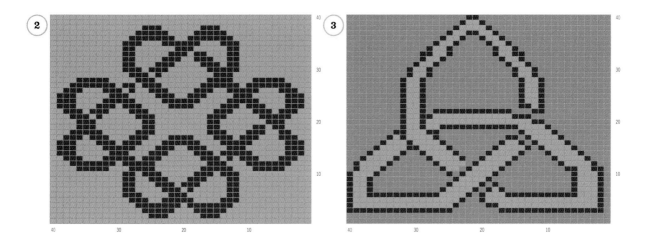

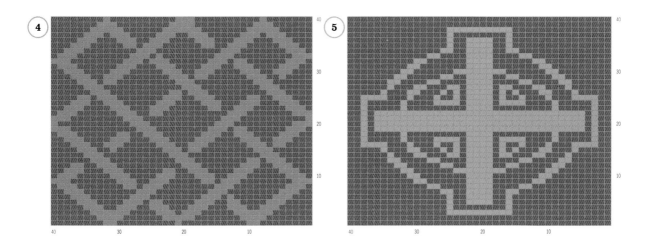

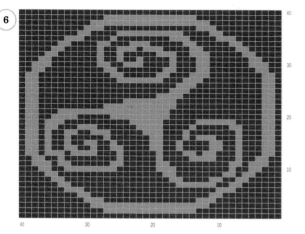

▼ *This is the symbol of the Triskelion. It has three spirals and can symbolise many things such as body, mind and spirit or Father, Son and Holy Ghost, but it is thought to originally symbolise The Great Mother, the lunar goddess who represents three lunar phases and has three personifications. Use separate bobbins of yarn or stranding to knit this motif (see page 236). Stranding (see page 239) will give a thicker finish but could work equally as well if you keep your floats loose and even.*

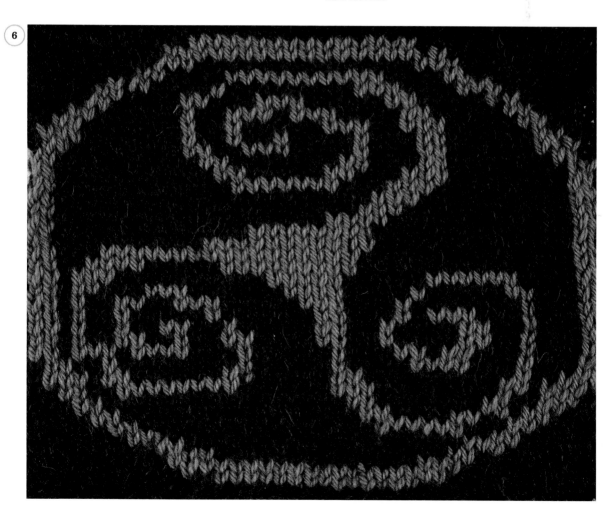

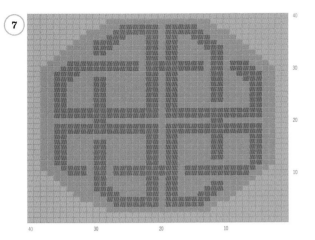

▼ *Knots are commonly seen in Celtic culture. Little is known about their origin; the first recorded knots date back to AD 450. They are said to represent the never-ending cycle of life. We cannot find a beginning or end in these knots so they are said to remind us of the timeless quality of life. Use bobbins of colour (see page 236) to work this motif or try stranding (see page 239) for a thicker finish. Keep floats loose and even if you use stranding.*

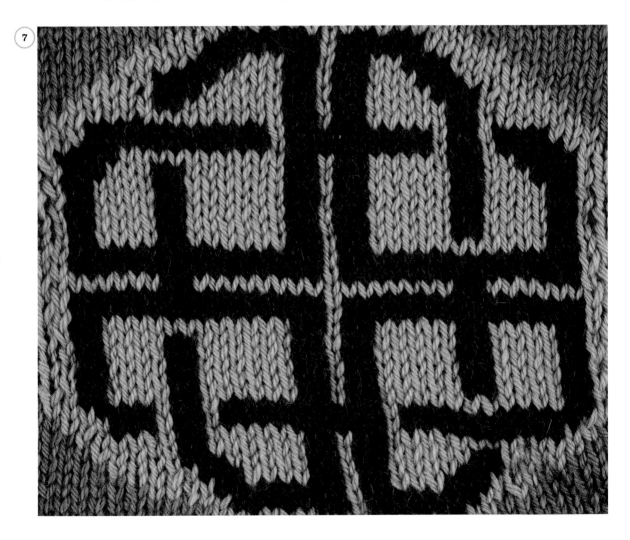

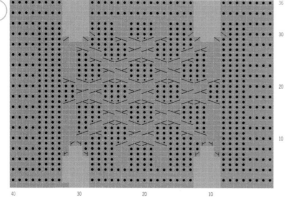

8

Key

- ● RS: purl WS: knit
- ◩ RS: m1 left leaning WS: m1 purlwise right leaning
- ◪ RS: m1 right leaning WS: m1 purlwise right leaning
- ◺ RS: ssk WS: p2tog tbl
- ◿ RS: k2tog WS: p2tog
- ☐ RS: Knit WS: Purl
- ⟩⟨ 2/2 LC
- ⟩⟨ 2/2 RC
- ⟩⟨ 2/2 RPC
- ⟩⟨ 2/2 LPC

40 sts x 40 sts

Rows 1–3: Knit. (40 sts)

Row 4: K12, p2, k4, p2, k12. (32 sts)

Row 5: K4, p8, k2, p4, k2, p8, k4.

Row 6: K8, m1pr, m1pl, (k4, p2) twice, k4, m1pr, m1pl, k8. (36 sts)

Row 7: K4, p4, k, p5, k2, p4, k2, p5, k, p4, k4.

Row 8: K8, p, m1pr, m1pl, k5, 2/2 RC, 2/2 LC, k5, m1pr, m1pl, p, k8. (40 sts)

Row 9: K4, p4, k2, p20, k2, p4, k4.

Row 10: K8, p2, 2/2 RPC, k4, 2/2 RC, k4, 2/2 LPC, p2, k8.

Row 11: Repeat row 9.

Row 12: K8, p2, k2, 2/2 RPC, 2/2 LC, 2/2 RC, 2/2 LPC, k2, p2, k8.

Row 13: Repeat row 9.

Row 14: K8, p2, (k4, 2/2 LC) twice, k4, p2, k8.

Row 15: Repeat row 9.

Row 16: K8, 2/2 RPC, (2/2 LC, 2/2 RC) twice, 2/2 LPC, k8.

Row 17: K4, p32, k4.

Row 18: K10, (2/2 RC, k4) twice, 2/2 RC, k10.

Row 19: Repeat row 17.

Row 20: K8, (2/2 LC, 2/2 RC) x 3, k8.

Row 21: Repeat row 9.

Row 22: Repeat row 14.

Row 23: Repeat row 9.

Row 24: K8, p2, k2, (2/2 LC, 2/2 RC) twice, k2, p2, k8.

Row 25: Repeat row 9.

Row 26: K8, p2, (2/2 RC, k4) twice, 2/2 RC, p2, k8.

Row 27: Repeat row 9.

Row 28: K8, p, p2tog tbl, k4, 2/2 LC, 2/2 RC, k4, p2tog, p, k8. (36 sts)

Row 29: K4, p3, ssk, k2tog, p3, k2, p4, k2, p3, ssk, k2tog, p3, k4. (32 sts)

Row 30: Repeat row 4.

Row 31: Repeat row 5.

Rows 32–35: Knit. (40 sts)

CIRCLES

Circles are everywhere, a continuous line with neither beginning nor end. What happens if we intersect them, join them, or even shatter them? This section explores all of these things and enhances the humble circle into something really special.

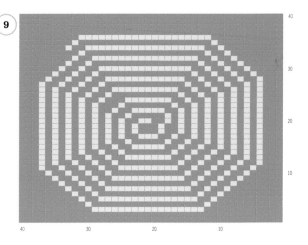

▼ Circles within circles make this fun to knit. Use stranding for this motif (see page 239) and for really small areas, you could even use Swiss darning (see page 241).

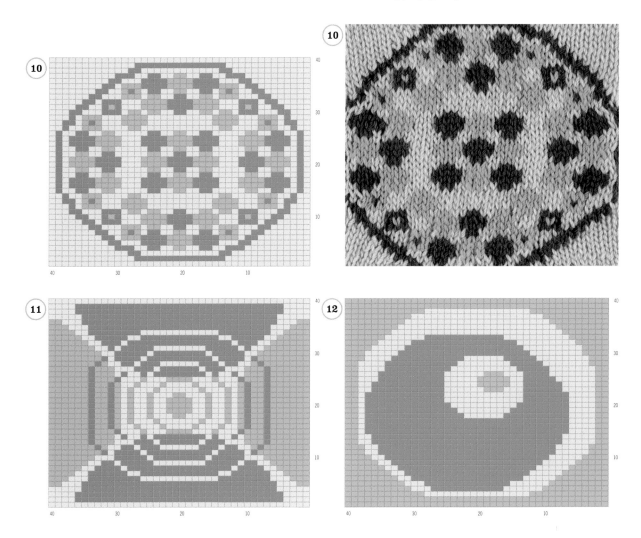

13

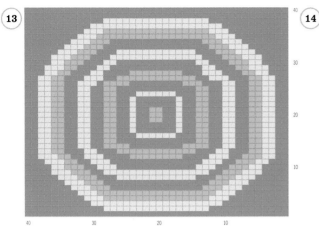

14

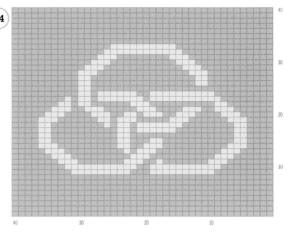

▼ *By intersecting circles, a pretty flower shape is created. For neat results, use separate bobbins to create this motif (see page 236).*

15

15

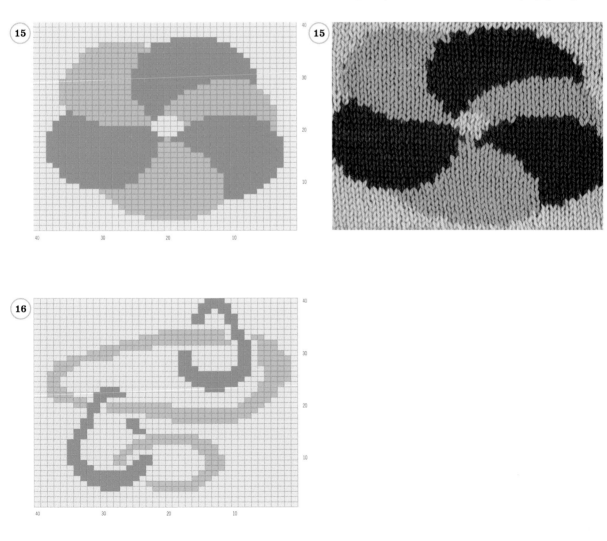

16

SQUARES

This section explores the humble square. More than just a border around the edge of a page, the square becomes exciting when turned on its point, bisected by other squares and challenged by the use of dominant and recessive colours.

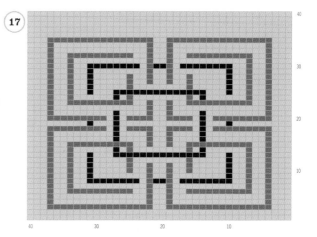

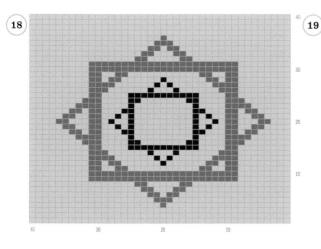

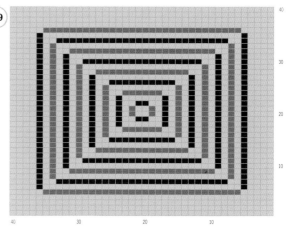

▼ The use of dominant and recessive colours here give this motif an 'op art' feel. The squares seem different sizes when turned on their side within the diamond shape. Use stranding to complete this motif (see page 239). You could even add beading to some of the square sides for extra sparkle (see page 249).

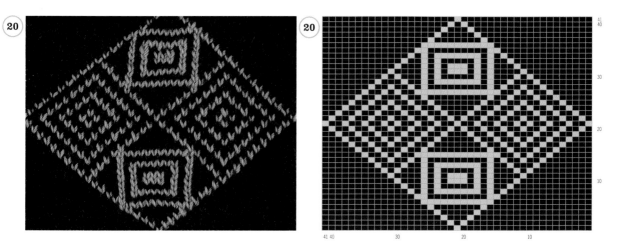

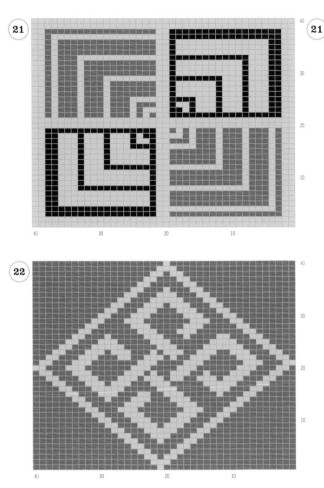

▲ *This motif shows what happens when you play with light and dark colours. The shapes are the same but the play between the colours really highlights the dominant and recessive qualities they have. It's a good lesson to use when designing patterns. Try substituting different colours and tones. It is surprising how colour can really change the mood of a design.*

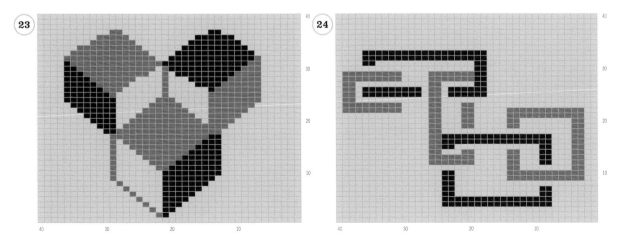

TRIANGLES

This section is an exploration of our trusty three-pointed friend, the triangle. Triangles tessellate beautifully when slotted together, but what happens when you change their angle from equilateral to right angled? Will they still fit, or can a beautiful new geometric pattern result?

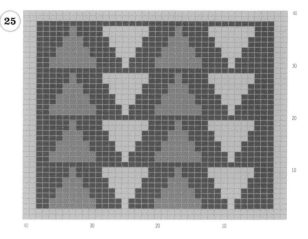

▼ *An all-over motif using just the one shape. However, use of colour within geometric designs really brings things to life. Light and dark shades give this a 3D-like appearance. The triangles almost become pyramids that lift off the page. Use bobbins of colour to complete this motif (see page 236).*

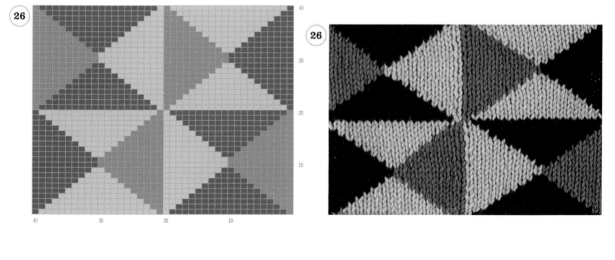

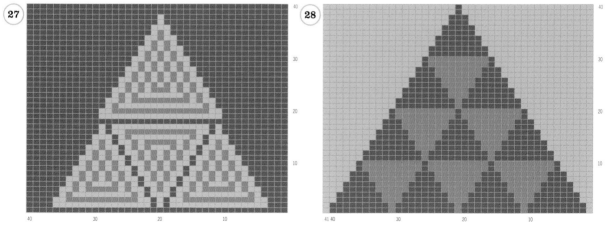

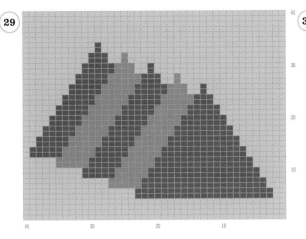

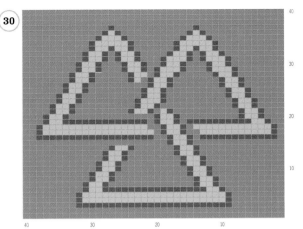

▼ *Assorted triangles fit neatly together within bigger triangles.*
Use bobbins of colour for the large triangles (see page 236). You could
even Swiss darn (see page 241) the smallest triangles afterwards to
make life easier.

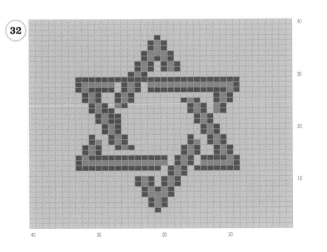

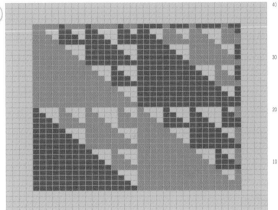

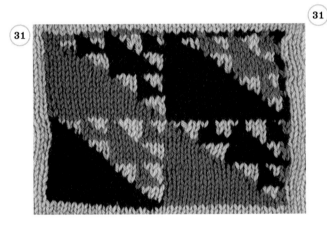

DIAMONDS

Is it a double triangle or a square on its side? Whatever it is, the diamond is an attractive and popular motif used in many cultures and commonly found throughout history. I've literally used diamonds to create a diamond motif in one of these designs. In others, I've explored the diamond's wonderful symmetry and form.

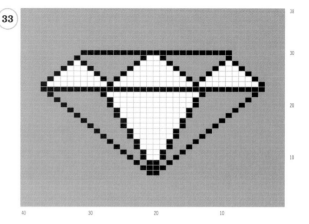

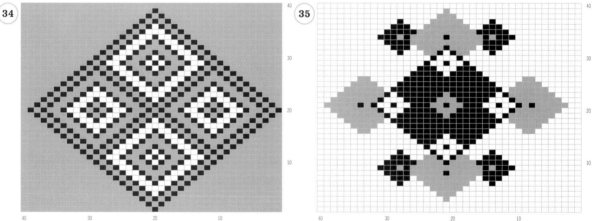

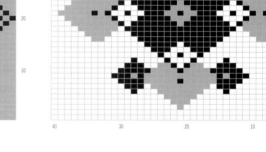

▼ This motif almost suggests a leaded glass design. Four smaller diamond panes are bisected by a larger central diamond motif. You could use beads to highlight the central diamond or work a raised purl stitch instead to add texture.

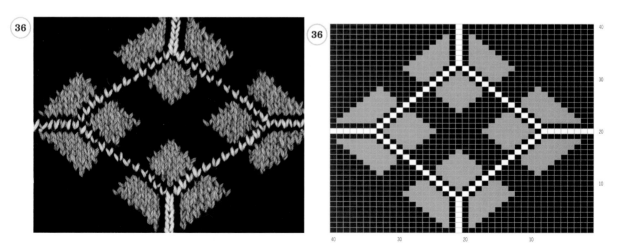

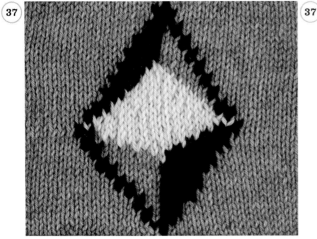

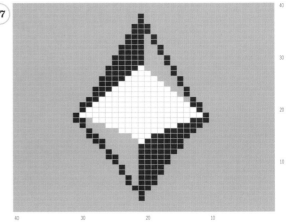

▲ The colours and size of diamonds used here definitely suggest a 3D motif. Is it flat or does it have sides and form? Use bobbins of colour for the best results when knitting this motif (see page 236).

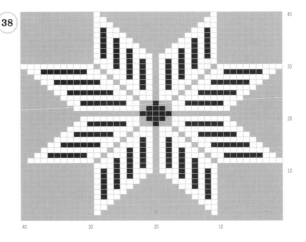

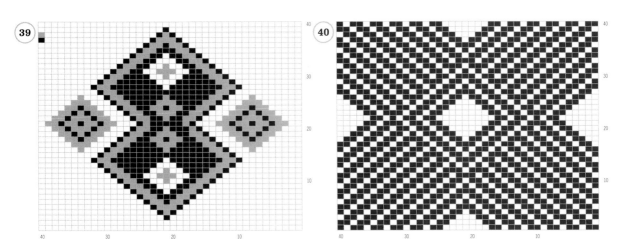

MULTI-SIDED

Not all geometric shapes are regular. Here I explore the many sided wonders that are all still geometrically beautiful. From pentagons to the plain abstract, I drew inspiration from diverse sources – from Art Deco designs to Native American art.

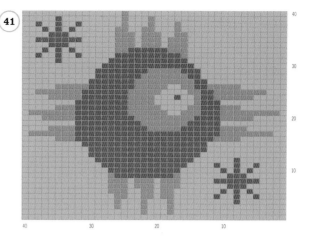

▼ *I love this little motif. Drawing inspiration from the Art Deco movement, these cute octagons are intersected by straight regular lines and circles. Use bobbins of yarn to work this motif (see page 236). The small circles at the centre of each octagon would be pretty if worked in beads or metallic yarn.*

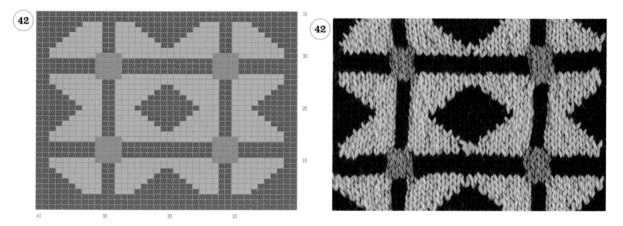

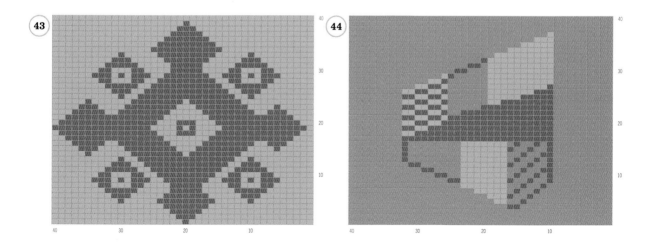

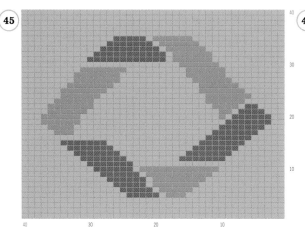

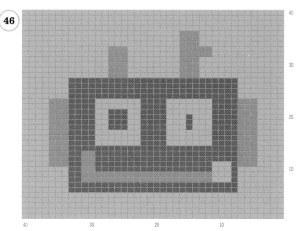

▼ *Again, Art Deco was my inspiration. I love the abstract quality of this motif. Use it to add some textural interest to a project.*

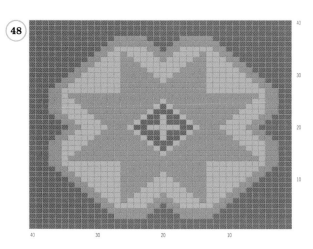

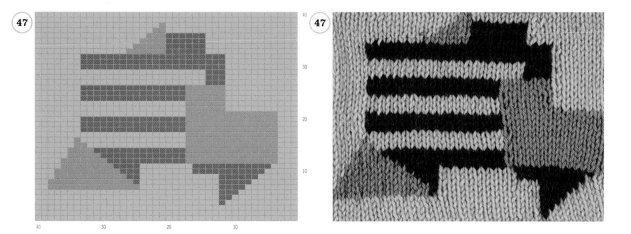

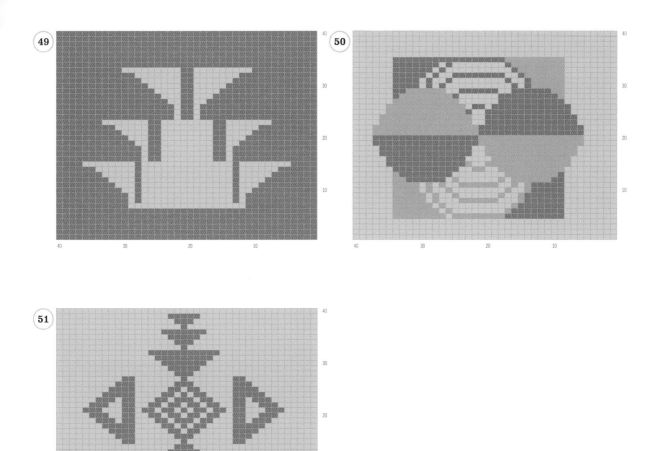

▼ I was inspired by Native American designs for this motif. Use bobbins to work this attractive geometric pattern (see page 236).

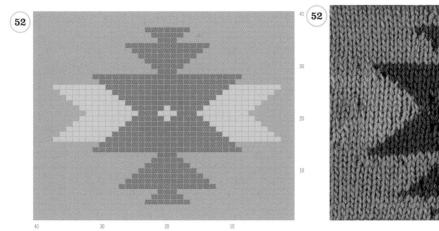

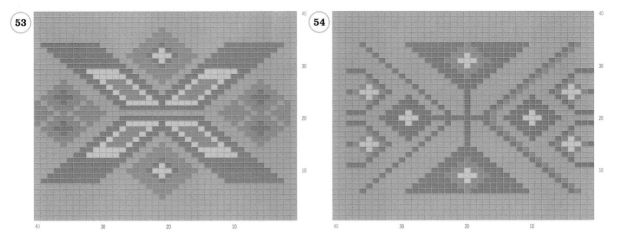

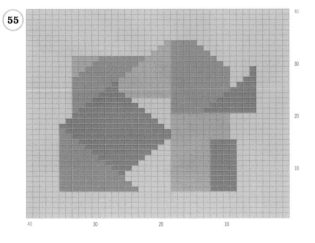

▼ This multisided motif uses abstract lines to break up and intersect the main shape. Use beads (see page 249) for some of the lines or add Swiss darning (see page 241) to them using different shades of yarn to create some extra texture.

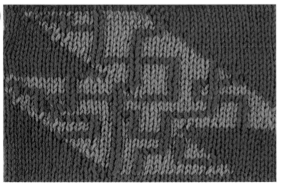

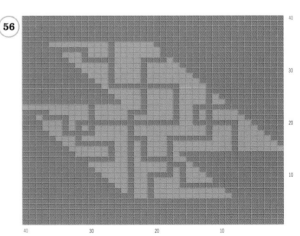

STARBURST

Starbursts are extremely dynamic. Think shooting stars across your work, exploding in a variety of colours and textures.

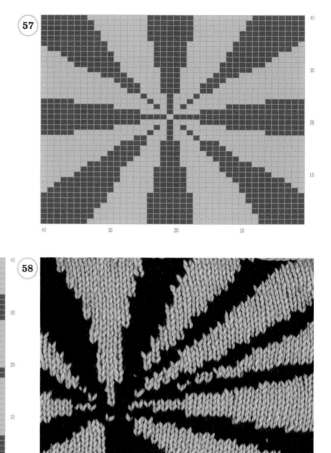

▲ Here the starburst from a corner of the motif extends upwards across the knitting. You could try knitting it in one colour, using a combination of knit and purl stitches for a textured look or brighten up the colour scheme by using a different shade for every ray.

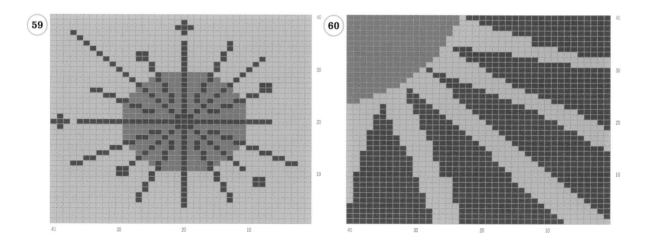

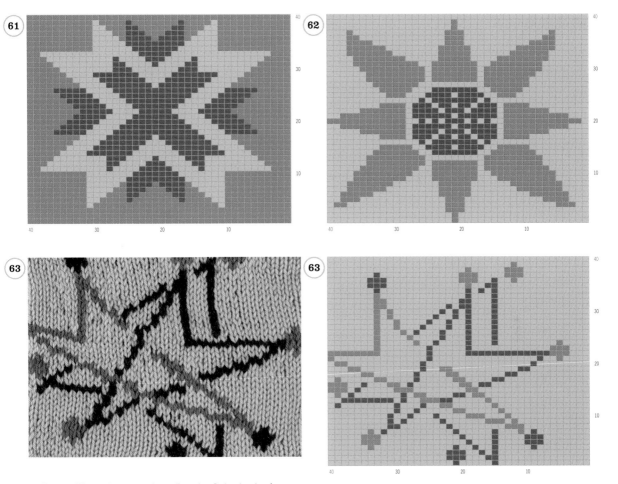

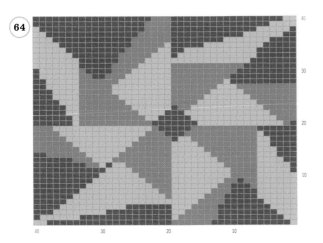

▲ This motif is an abstract starburst. Try using Swiss darning (see page 241) to embroider the motif on after knitting one solid colour block. Add sequins and beads for a truly dynamic flourish.

HEARTS

So you think you know what a heart looks like? Well, in this section I see what a heart can do when it wants to play with geometrics. I've turned the heart upside down and inside out in my quest for unusual and interesting patterns.

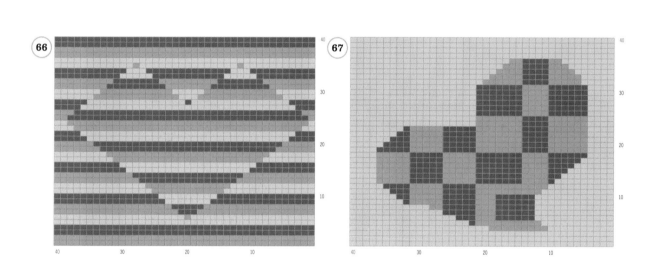

▼ Inspired by patchwork quilts, this heart is made from triangles and diamonds. Use blocks of colour to work this motif. A strong design, this would be great centred on a bag or an afghan block.

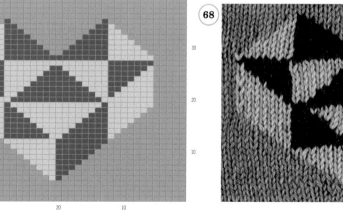

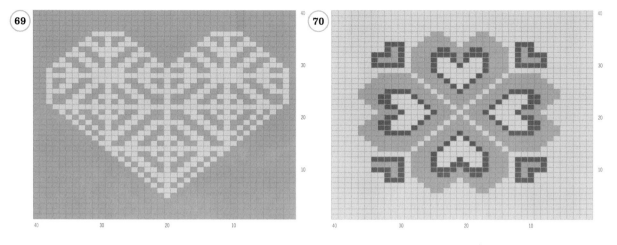

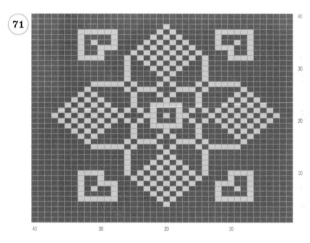

▼ Just for fun, I turned the heart upside down and filled it with more hearts. A mix of stranding (see page 239) and bobbins of colour (see page 236) would work here. Add beads too if you are feeling adventurous (see page 249).

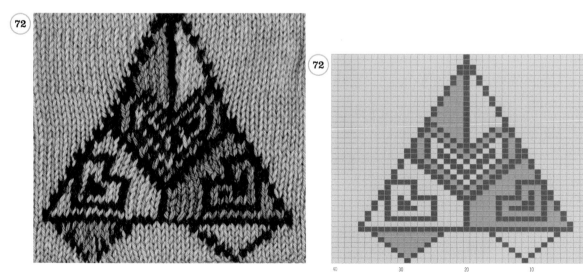

ASIAN

I used symbols and motifs commonly found in rugs from the Far and Middle East for this section. Each motif has a meaning that reaches far back into history and made me look again at common patterns found on these beautiful textiles.

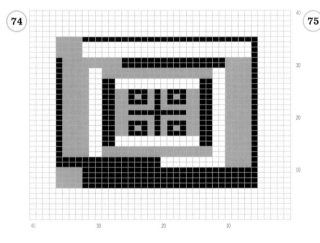

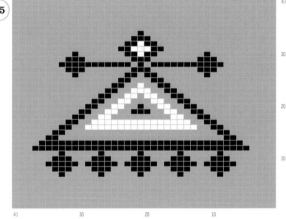

▼ *This motif represents the scorpion and is a common symbol found on Eastern rugs. For nomads, the scorpion is deadly if it enters your tent. It is believed the scorpion will not cross a rug with the scorpion symbol on it, thus providing protection from its deadly sting. Use small bobbins of colour for this motif and add beads to the centre for texture.*

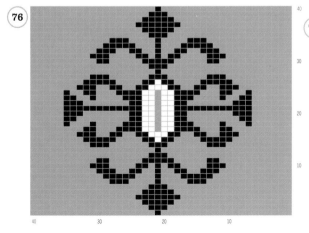

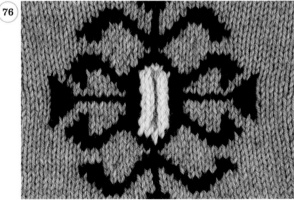

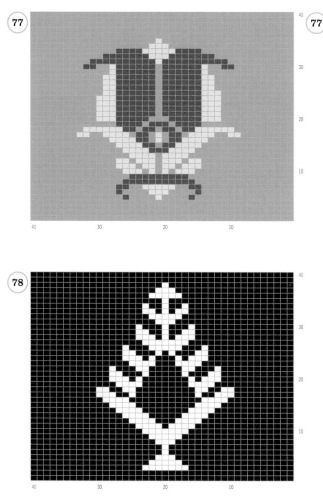

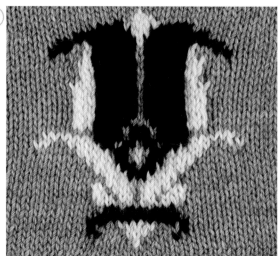

▲ *The lotus flower is a sacred Asian motif. It is said to have its roots in mud and dirt while its blossom points heavenward. Use blocks of colour to knit this attractive and strong motif. Why not try knitting these motifs into blocks for an oriental rug of your own?*

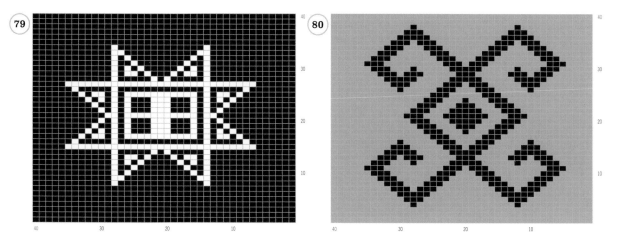

NORWEGIAN SNOWFLAKE

This is one of the best-known knitting motifs ever, in my humble opinion. With its origins rooted in traditional Norwegian knitting, the snowflake shape is easily recognisable and much copied. Here I have tried to explore variations on this theme.

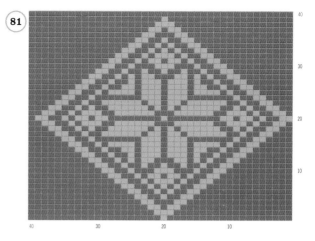

▼ *A typical snowflake design with the ice crystals reaching out in a feather pattern from each corner. Use stranding (see page 239) to work this pretty motif.*

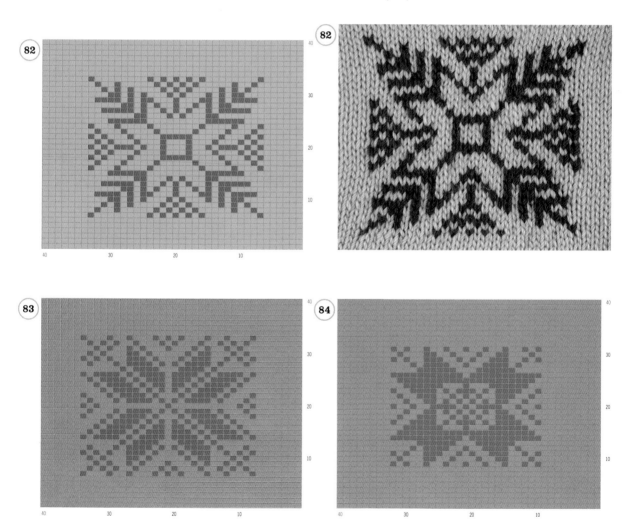

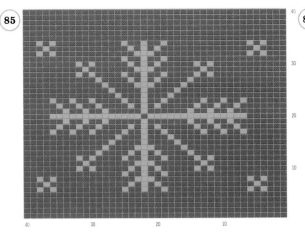

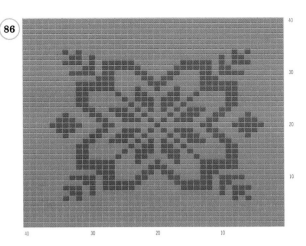

▼ This snowflake is slightly different because of its cross-like nature. Smaller snowflakes surround the central large one while checked bands hug the middle. Again, stranding (see page 239) is the best technique to use as only two colours are ever used per row.

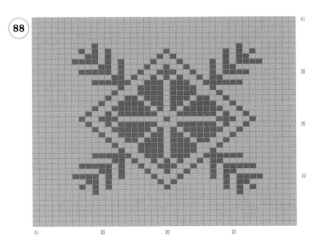

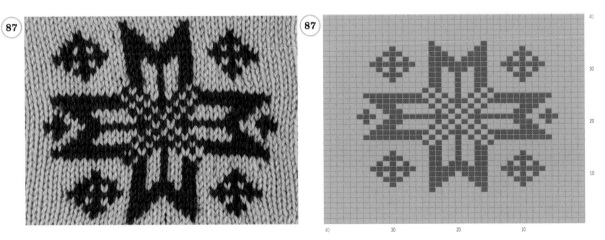

MONSTER TOY

This cute monster toy is easy to make. It's a great project for practising Fair Isle technique. His sweater features one of the motifs from this chapter. You could try substituting any of the motifs for a different look. Why not play with colours here too to make your monster truly personal?

Key

☐ RS: Knit WS: Purl

▨ Grasshopper

▩ Apple

▨ Mustard

■ Cocoa Bean

☑ RS: Knit into fb WS: Purl into fb

▨ Grey no stitch

◹ RS: k2tog WS: p2tog

◺ RS: ssk WS: p2tog tbl

MATERIALS:

Rowan Pure Wool Worsted

1 × 100g (219 yds) balls each in shades Ivory (A), Moonstone (B), Apple (C), Cocoa Bean (D), Grasshopper (E), Mustard (F)

Rowan Kidsilk Haze

2 × 25g (229 yds) ball in shade Jelly (optional)

4mm (US 6) straight needles

4mm (US 6) dpns

Polyester toy stuffing

Small piece of grey and white felt.

1 large black button/1 small green button for eye

1 small black button/1 small green button for eye on sweater

Tapestry needle

Sewing needle and matching thread.

TENSION

A precise tension is not essential for this project

MEASUREMENTS

Monster is approx. 38cm (15in) tall by 25cm (10in) wide

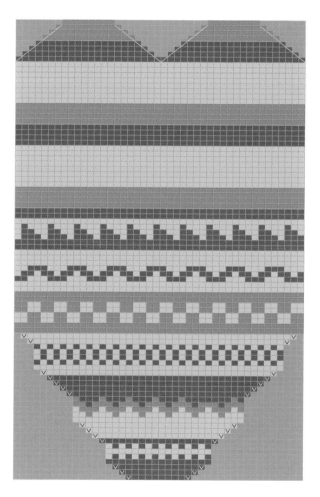

MONSTER SWEATER:

Front:

Using 4mm (US 6) straight needles, CO 40 sts in A.

Work 4 rows in stocking stitch.

Work 4 rows in k2/p2 rib.

Work 2 rows in stocking stitch.

Using Chart 41 from this chapter, work from row 2 to the end of the chart. If you prefer a textured look to your monster, work the main body of the monster motif in 1 strand C plus 2 strands Kidsilk Haze knitted together. I used B for the tentacles and eye.

After working the chart, change to A and work 2 rows in stocking stitch.

Work 4 rows in k2/p2 rib.

Work 4 rows in stocking stitch.

Cast off loosely knitwise.

Back:

Work as front of sweater but instead of working the 38 rows of the chart, work 38 rows of stocking stitch using A.

FINISHING

Weave in loose yarn ends and block and steam pieces into shape.

Sew side seams leaving a 4cm (1½in) opening on each side just below the top k2/p2 rib for armholes.

ARMHOLES

Using 4mm (US 6) and with RS facing, pick up and knit 24 sts around armhole. Work k2/p2 for 4 rounds. Cast off loosely in rib.

Repeat for second armhole.

Darn in loose yarn ends.

Using a sewing needle and matching thread, sew on two buttons for the monster's eye as shown in the photo.

MONSTER TOY:

Front and Back (alike):

Using D and 4mm (US 6) straight needles, CO 10 sts.

Work from chart until complete.

Arms: make 2

Using B and 4mm (US 6) dpns, CO 6 sts.

Divide the stitches across three needles with 2 sts on each.

Join the round and knit 1 round.

Working a knit round every time, increase as folls:

R1: kfb, k to end of needle (rep 3 times).

Rep this round until you have 10 sts on all three needles (30 sts).

Work three rounds even.

Decrease as folls:

Round 1: k2tog, k to end of needle (rep 3 times).

Rep this round until you have 4 sts on all three needles (12sts).

Divide the sts on two needles, i.e: 6 sts per needles.

Work even until arm meas 20cm (8in).

Cast off.

Turn whole arm WS out so the reverse stocking stitch side is outermost.

Weave in loose yarn ends

Stuff the hand part of the arm firmly with toy stuffing.

FINISHING

Weave in loose ends. Block and steam pieces into shape.

Pin the arms in place to the front of one of the pieces. With the arms enclosed in the middle of the sandwich, place the second monster piece on top making sure the RS are facing each other.

Sew around the edges using back stitch. Leave a small opening along the side edge of the monster for turning and stuffing.

Turn monster RS out and stuff firmly.

Close the opening with small, firm stitches.

Eye:

Cut out a 10cm (4in) diameter circle in grey felt.

Cut out a 5cm (2in) diameter circle in white felt.

Pin the grey circle in place using the photo as a guide. Using a sewing needle and matching thread, sew the circle in place using a small back stitch around the outer edge. Place the white circle over the top as in the photo and sew this in place as before.

Sew the black button firmly in place.

Sew the green button firmly in place over the top.

7

ALL-OVER REPEATS

In this chapter we explore the geometric form in a series of all-over repeat patterns. What this means for you as a knitter is that whatever the size of your project, providing you do the maths, you could potentially use any of these patterns to enhance or alter the mood of your work. I have spread the net wide and used influences from traditional historical knitted patterns, the Celts, Scandinavia and the Middle East, as well as more abstract references to give added interest and visual appeal.

FAIR ISLE

We briefly touched on Celtic art as a motif in Chapter 6. Here we go farther and develop the knots and spirals into all-over patterns.

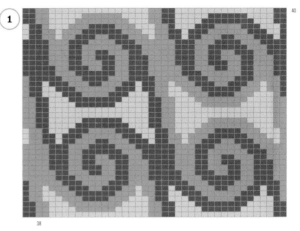

▼ *Nature features heavily in Celtic art and symbols. Here leaves and vines twist and ramble across the work. Use stranding to work this swatch (see page 236) and you could add a contrast thread to work the veins of leaves using back stitch.*

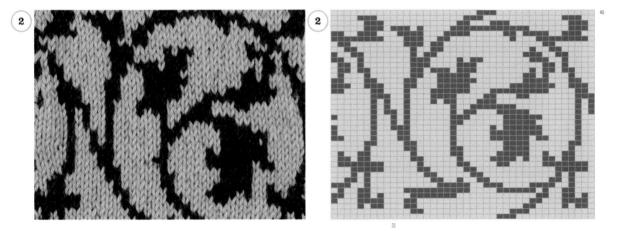

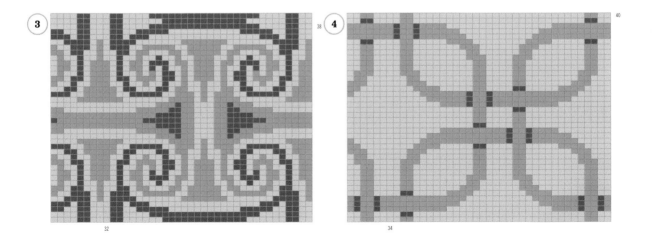

5

5

36

40

▲ *This repeat is best worked using the stranding method (see page 239). Either work things as they are and cover your knitting with the cross-shaped knot or isolate one repeat and work as a single motif.*

6

39

30

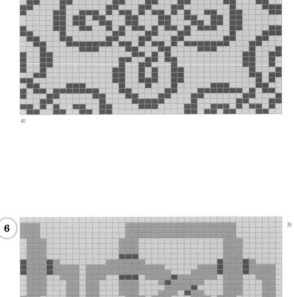

7

40

8

20

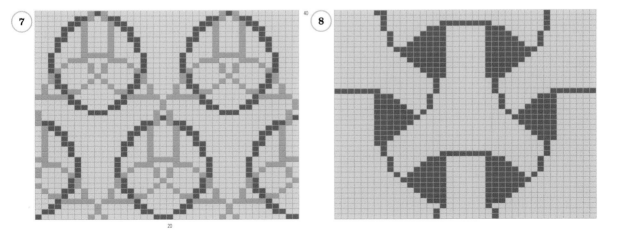

72

12

9

◄ *Use stranding (see page 239) to achieve this compact repeat, which is similar in appearance to the Greek Key pattern. This would be a great covering for a bag or even as an edging when used against a bigger and bolder pattern as in swatch 10.*

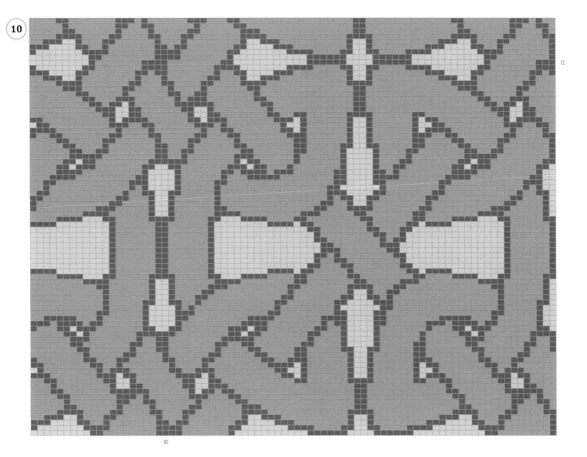

72

60

◄ *These big, bold knots, although effective, are definitely a more complex knit. Use a mix of stranding (see page 239) and bobbins (see page 236) to achieve this design. Plan it out carefully beforehand and if you want to make life easier, why not Swiss darn (see page 241) the smaller areas of dark green at the end?*

SCANDINAVIA ¹¹

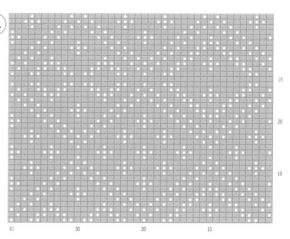

Again, we touched on the motifs of Scandinavia in Chapter 6. But with a rich historical tradition of knitted colour work, I couldn't resist a deeper look at some of the geometric patterns familiar to this region.

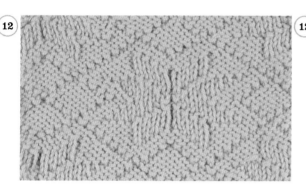

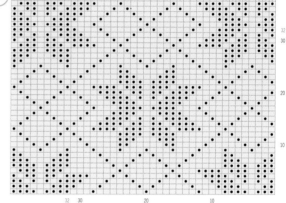

▲ *The use of relief stitches, i.e. knit and purl with one colour yarn ,is known as damask knitting. It has deep roots in tradition and early samples of damask knitting have been found and recorded from all over the world. Here I have used the traditional Norwegian rose pattern and worked it into an all-over damask repeat pattern.*

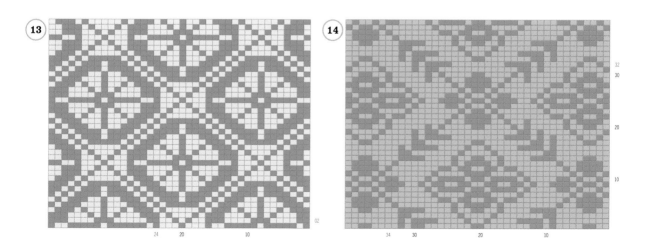

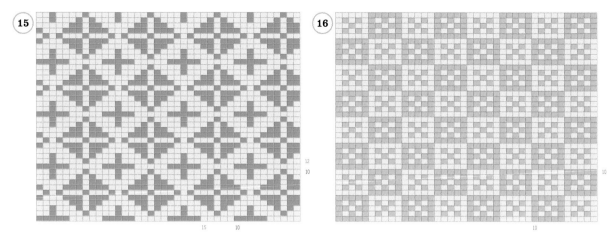

15

16

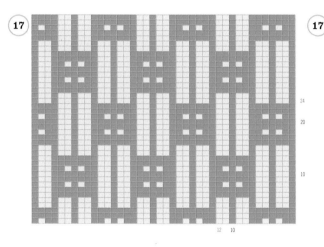

17

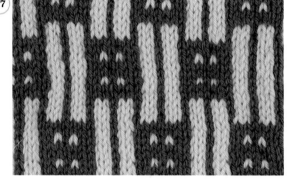

17

▲ *A step away from the better-known snowflake and rose type designs much used by many knitters, this geometric block and line pattern is bold and edgy. Use stranding (see page 239) to work this pattern and make a statement.*

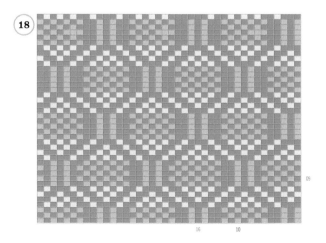

18

HISTORICAL PATTERNS

The tradition of knitting goes back many thousands of years, with the first recorded samples of knitted socks found in Syria before the time of Christ. I have derived much pleasure in taking a walk across the world to capture a selection of traditional historical patterns familiar to different regions and eras.

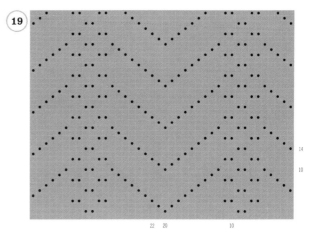

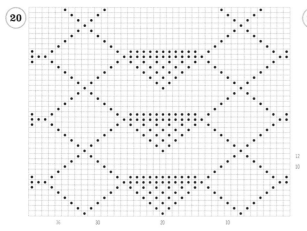

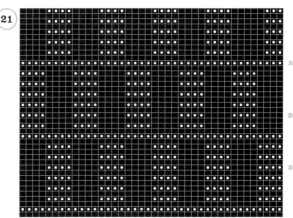

▼ This blockwork pattern is knitted in relief using a combination of knit and purl stitches. It is a traditional repeat used commonly on the fishermen's ganseys found around the ports of the UK. The gansey sweater was knitted with 5ply yarn on small needles to form a tightly woven garment which kept the water out. The patterns across the chest depicted waves, ropes, sand and chains. Patterns appear to be unique to their owners, with everything knitted from memory and passed from knitter to knitter.

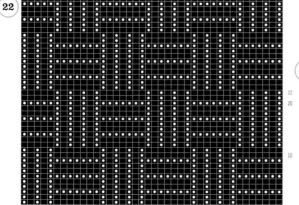

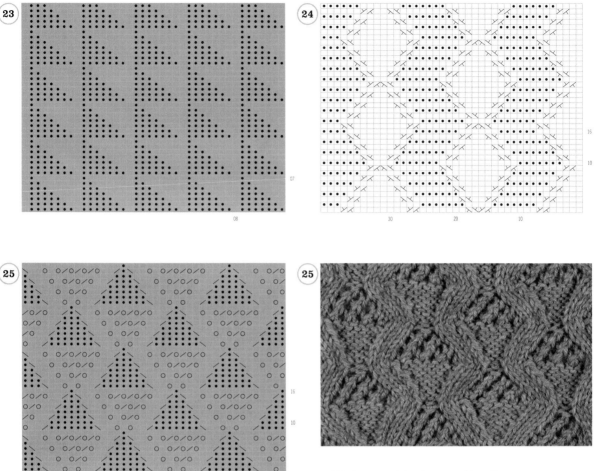

▲ This lace repeat is inspired by traditional Shetland lace knitting. Shetland lace is renowned throughout the world for its beautiful lace detailing and gossamer-fine finish. It is said a Shetland Hap shawl should be fine enough to be passed through a wedding ring. Knitted with very fine lace-weight yarn and then blocked into shape on large wooden frames, these shawls gave the island women of Shetland a living for many years.

27

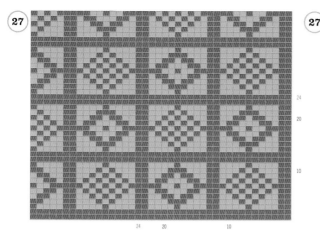

27

▲ *Sanquhar is a town located in Dumfries and Galloway in Scotland. Knitting subsidised the meagre living gained from subsistence farming. Sanquhar knitting is distinctive in that it uses two colours, usually black and white, and traditional monochrome geometric patterns such as midge and fly, the duke, trellis, rose, and here, the drum pattern. Stockings and gloves were commonly knitted using these patterns. Stranding works well for these repeats (see page 239).*

28

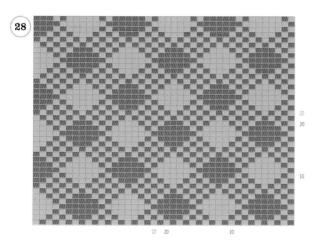

29

30

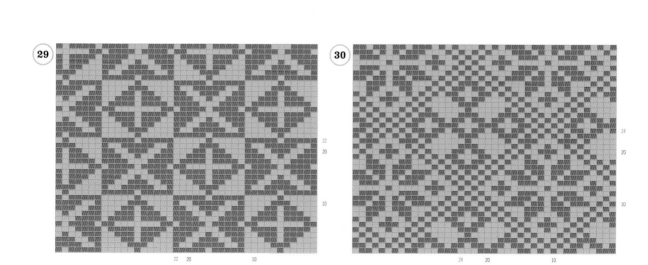

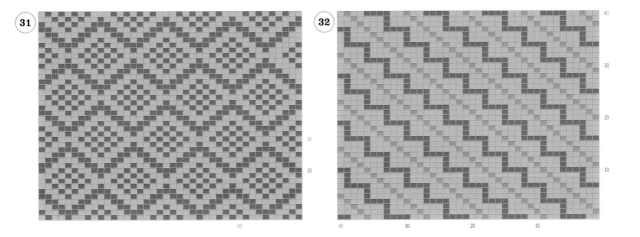

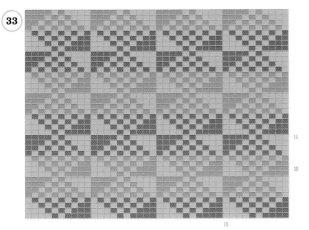

▼ *I couldn't resist this unusual Scandinavian repeat. An interesting play on diamonds, it is best worked using the stranding technique (see page 239). This would be fantastic worked over a sweater with contrast welts.*

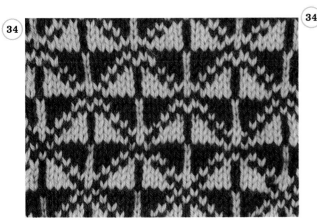

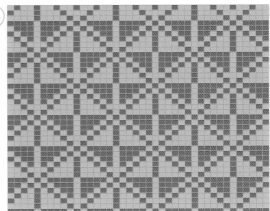

MIDDLE EASTERN

For this section, I researched the beautifully rich art and culture of Turkey, Persia, Syria and the Islamic tradition, to name but a few. From carpets to mosaic tiles, the geometric patterns used are breathtaking and timeless. On closer inspection, though, similar shapes and themes are found in slightly different forms within Middle Eastern art and I have tried to capture the familiar ones here.

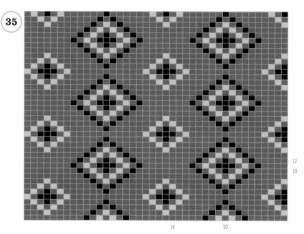

▼ *This curved trident pattern is commonly seen in both rugs and tiles within Middle Eastern culture. Use stranding (see page 239) to work this repeat.*

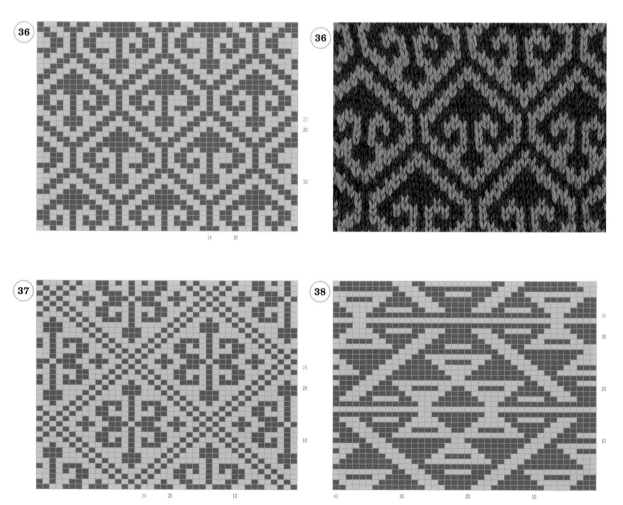

39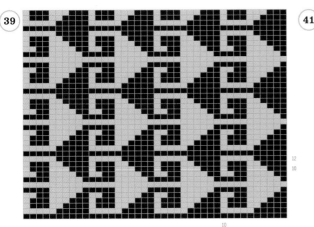

41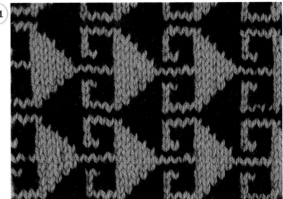

▲ *Here we see the curved trident shape again, although this time running sideways. It is a good example of how recurrent shapes and motifs are worked in different ways throughout the art of this region. Use stranding (see page 239) for best results.*

40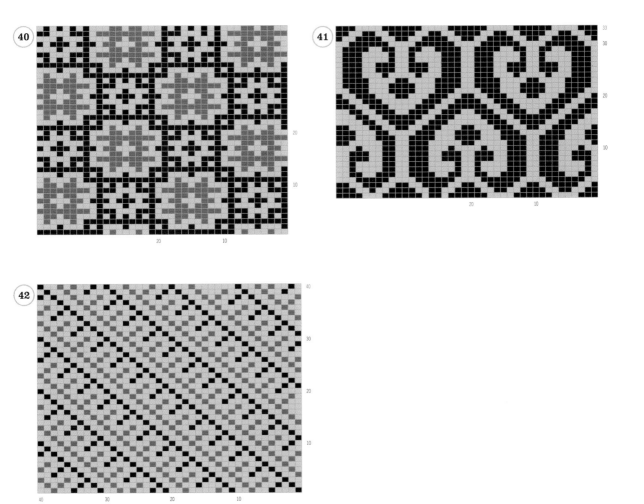

41

42

28
20
10

20   10

43

◄ *Using dark and light tones of the same colour gives damask-like effect to patterns such as these. Use stranding (see page 239) to achieve best results. Don't be afraid to experiment with colour too. Three colours or more could be used here to give dramatically different results.*

44

◀ A variation of the same shapes and patterns found in Chart 43. Play with colours and try adding a shot of metallic gold yarn with rich plums and damsons for a more opulent feel. Give it your own taste of pomegranates and cinnamon spices.

RANDOM/ ABSTRACT

This was a great opportunity to play with geometrics. I referred to the Art Deco and Art Noveau periods of art culture as well as dabbling with designs from the 1950s and 1960s. Stop here to find a pattern to give a contemporary feel to any of your knitted projects.

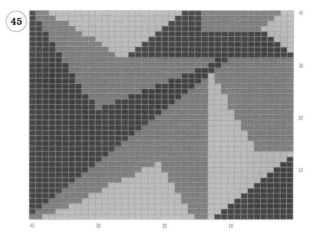

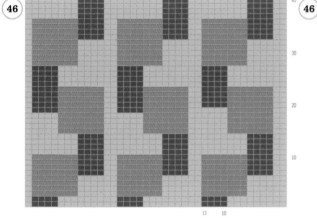

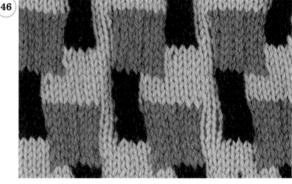

▲ *I love this repeat. It reminds me of the textile patterns found in the 1950s. Knit it up as a cushion cover or retro afghan. Use bobbins of colour (see page 236) to achieve this effect.*

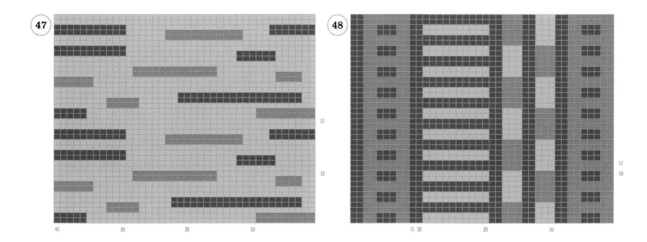

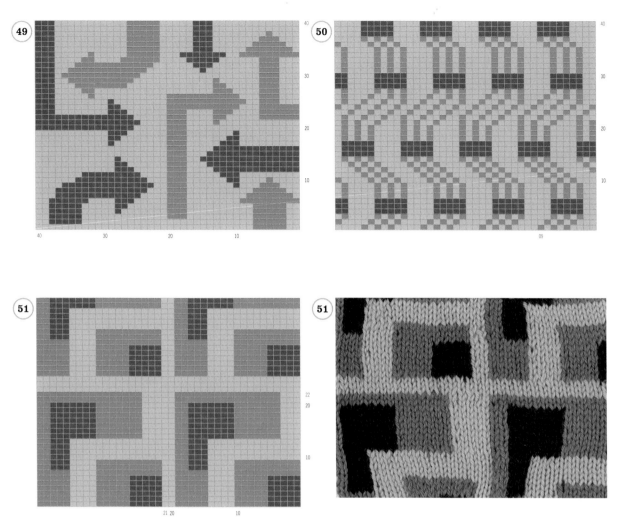

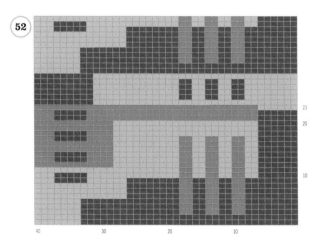

▲ *A hark back to the wonderful Art Deco era. Use this for homewares or make swatches in this and also Chart 46 before stapling to a canvas board and using as wall hangings. Use bobbins of colour (see page 236) to knit this repeat.*

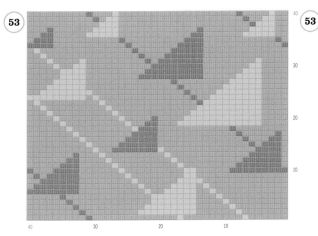

53

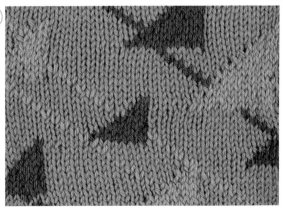

53

▲ *Dynamic triangles run randomly along diagonal lines and are almost dart-like in appearance. Hot clashing colours give this 1960s appeal while monochrome colours would swing the date right back to the 1920s. Use bobbins (see page 236) of yarn for this repeat.*

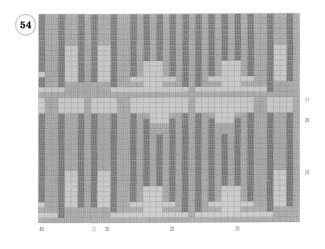

54

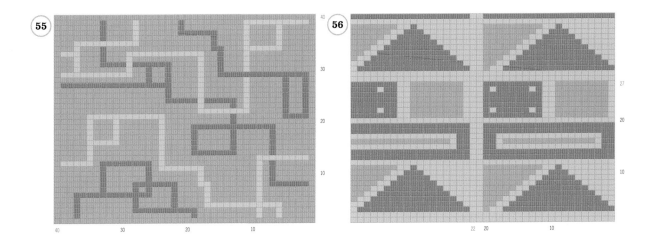

55

56

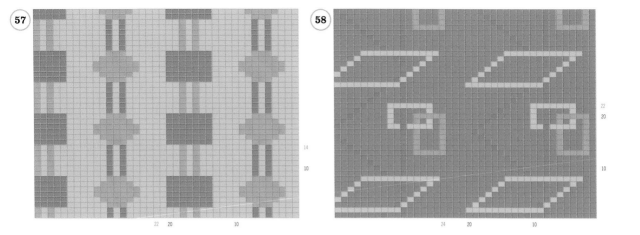

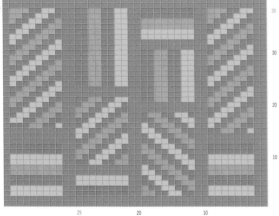

▼ Squares of fun dominate this pattern repeat. I have mixed up the colours here for a lively effect but keeping to two colours would change the mood entirely. Stranding (see page 239) would be the easiest way to tackle things here.

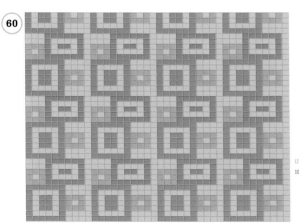

SYMMETRICAL (61)

The very nature of geometry breeds symmetry in many cases. Here I have tried to capture a little symmetry in an all-over repeat. Interestingly, some well-known shapes and patterns, such as the national flag of the UK, are symmetrical. Have a look around for examples of everyday symmetry that could inspire you.

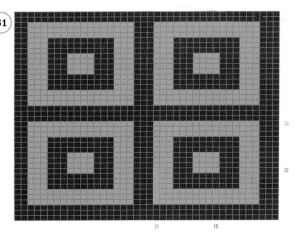

▼ *The triangles of this all-over repeat run in opposite directions, which gives rise to a vertical line of symmetry. If you were to fold the pattern horizontally, you would still get the same symmetry but the colours would be opposite to each other, rather like a negative photograph. Stranding (see page 239) would be the best option for this pattern.*

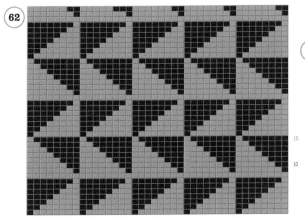

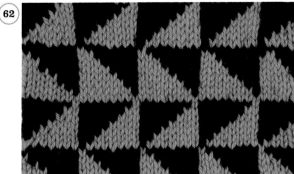

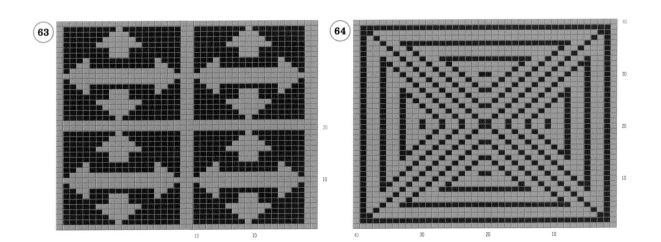

65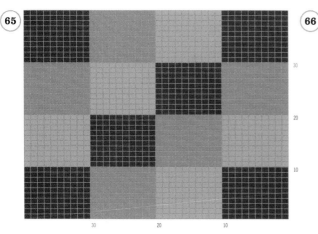

66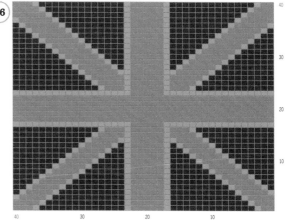

▼ *I have had fun with these squares and diamonds, twisting and turning and adding bold colour options. Symmetry is apparent in every direction here. Use bobbins of colour (see page 236) to knit up this bold explosion. Work as a repeat or as a standalone motif, which could be great used for an afghan block.*

67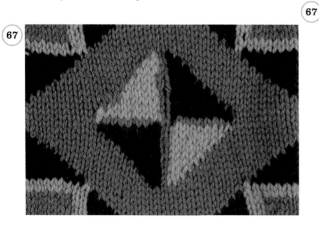

67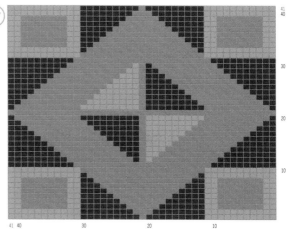

68

BEADED FAIR ISLE BAG

Worked in bright neons and using beads and stranding yarns to make the Fair Isle pattern, this little bag completely updates the traditional image of Fair Isle knitting.

YARN
Rico Fashion Pixel: 1 × 50g (128 yds) ball in 001 A
Rowan Cotton Glace: 1 × 50g (125 yds) ball in Shoot (814) B

BEADS
Size 6 glass beads: 126 in blue and 111 in orange

TOOLS
Pair of 3.25mm (US 3) circular needle or dpns
Blunt tapestry needle
Stitch marker

TENSION
26 sts and 28 rows to 10cm (4in) using 3.25mm (US 3) needles and measured over st st

MEASUREMENTS
11 × 13cm (4 × 5in)

ABBREVIATIONS
PB = place bead using slip stitch technique (see page 249)

BAG
Thread 108 blue beads onto yarn A and the remaining 18 beads onto yarn B.

Using yarn A, cast on 60 sts, distributing sts evenly over dpns and taking care not to twist when joining in the round. Place marker to denote beg of round.

Rounds 1–5: Knit.
Rounds 6–16: Work Chart A, rep 6 times around.
Rounds 17–21: Knit.

Break yarn A and thread all orange beads onto yarn A.

Rounds 22–30: Work Chart B, rep 15 times around.
Rounds 31–35: Knit.

Join in yarn B, but do not break yarn A.

Rounds 36–44: Work Chart C, rep 6 times around.

Note: On round 45 you will need to carry yarn B and place blue bead as indicated on the chart.

Rounds 45–49: Knit.
Round 50: Purl.
Rounds 51–55: Knit.

Cast off.

FINISHING

Fold bound-off edge to the WS at ridge (round 50) and slip-stitch edge to WS of knitting using yarn A. Fold knitting flat and sew up cast-on edge to make bag.

Cut two 50cm (20in) lengths of yarn A and twist them together to make a cord or cut three lengths and braid them into a cord. Make a second cord the same way. Using the large-eyed needle, thread one cord from the RS through the knitting into the channel, on a side edge. Thread it right around the channel and out where it came in. Knot the ends together. Repeat the process with the other cord, starting and ending on the opposite side edge.

CHART A

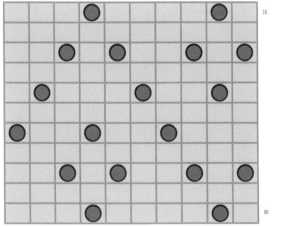

Key

▢ 001

▢ Shoot

CHART B

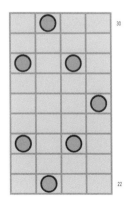

CHART C

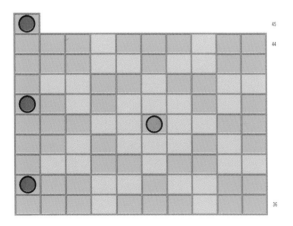

8

MANIPULATED FABRICS

This chapter deals with ways of creating textural pattern on knitted fabrics, so the charts have keys for different stitches. Some also feature colourwork. Note that on many of these charts you need a set-up row and edge stitches. These are given on the charts, so row 1 won't always be the first row shown. The right-hand edge stitches are given, then the pattern repeat, and you can reverse the edge stitches to neatly finish the left edge if need be.

SLIP STITCH COLOUR

These patterns are very easy to work, and sometimes wonderfully surprising in the effects they produce. Most of the repeats are short, so you quickly get into the rhythm, and slip stitch is a very simple form of colour knitting. It is ideal for novice knitters looking to move on from working in plain colours.

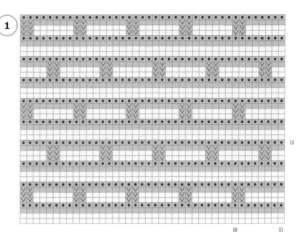

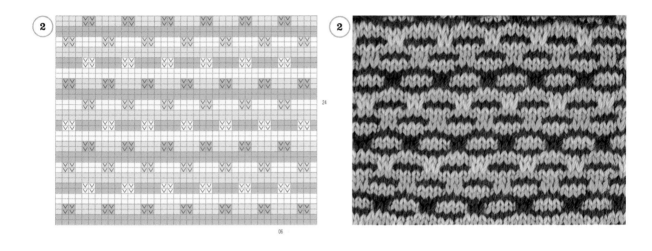

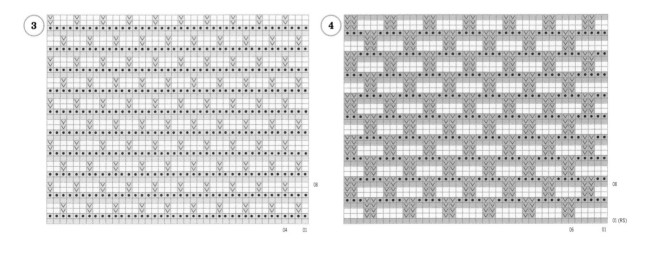

Key

☐ knit on RS, purl on WS

⊡ purl on RS, knit on WS

☑ s1 pwise wyif: slip 1 stitch purlwise with yarn at front of work

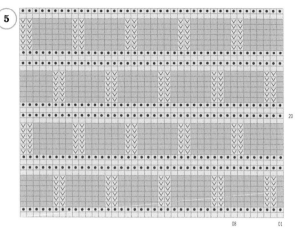

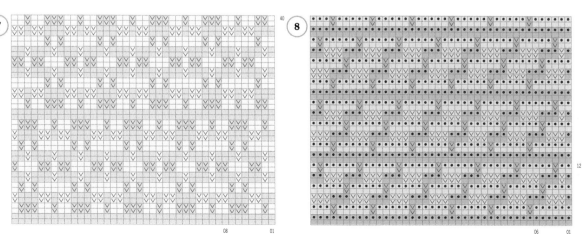

SLIP STITCH TEXTURE

Slip stitch knitting offers a simple way of creating elaborate-looking texture, as well as colour patterns (see page 242). Some patterns are reversible, making them ideal for scarves and even throws, though the knitted fabric can be quite thick and stiff.

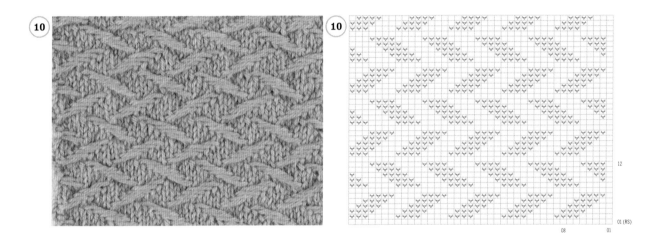

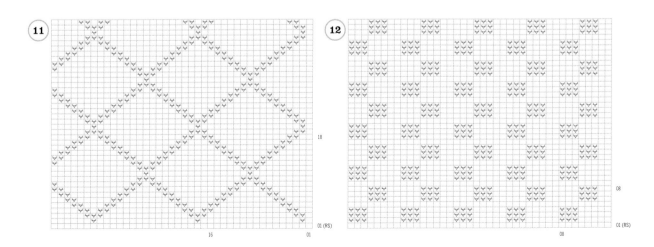

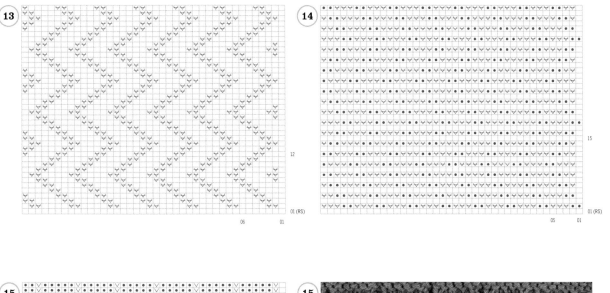

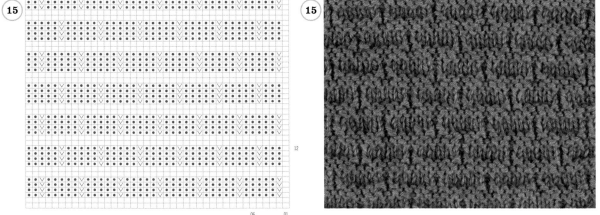

Key

☐ knit on RS, purl on WS

⊡ purl on RS, knit on WS

☑ s1 pwise wyif: slip 1 stitch purlwise with yarn at front of work

☑ s1 pwise wyib: slip 1 stitch purlwise with yarn at back of work

MOSAIC PATTERNS

This is a popular style of colour slip stitch knitting that produces intricate designs incredibly simply. You are only ever working with one colour at a time, so do try out some of these patterns if you are new to colour knitting; they are easy and relatively quick to work.

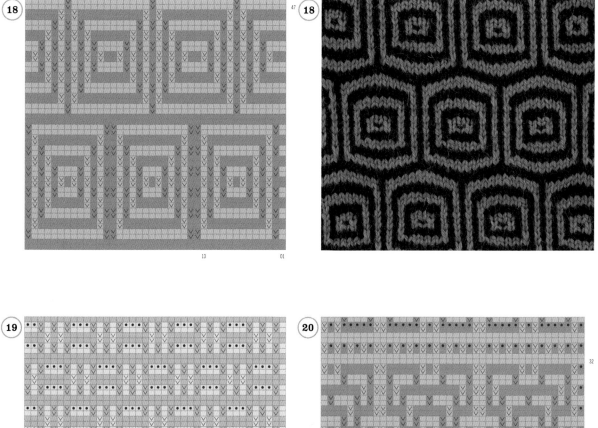

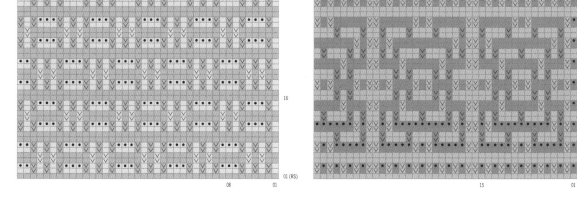

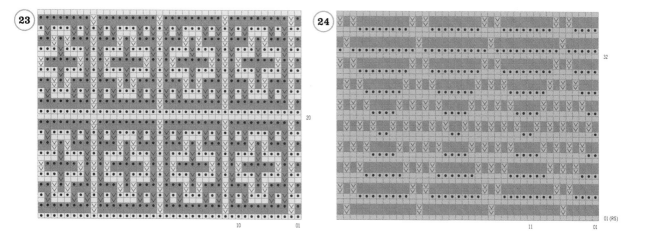

21

21

22

23

24

Key

☐ knit on RS, purl on WS

⊡ purl on RS, knit on WS

☑ s1 pwise wyif: slip 1 stitch purlwise with yarn at front of work

☒ s1 pwise wyib: slip 1 stitch purlwise with yarn at back of work

WRAPPED STITCHES

These charts all involve wrapping the working yarn around strands of stitches to create textural patterns. These are not quick fabrics to work, but they aren't difficult either, and the patterns can be used as panels or feature detailing on otherwise plain projects if you don't want an all-over texture

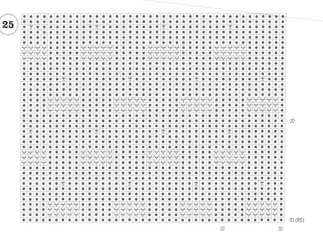

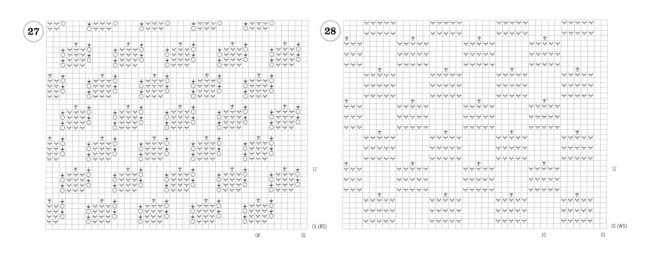

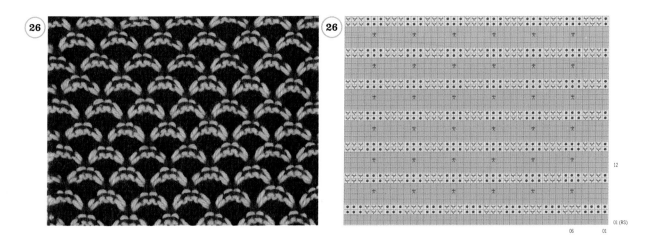

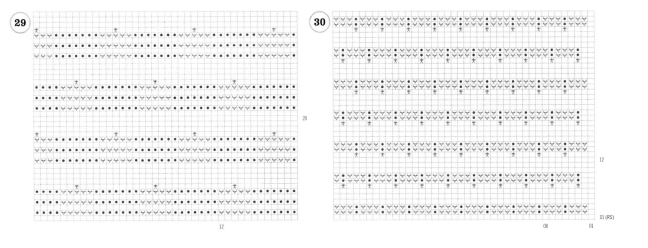

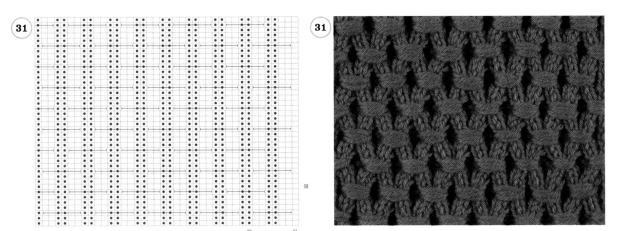

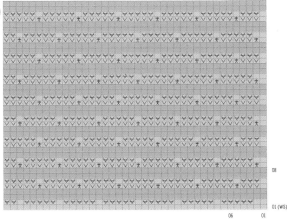

Key

- ☐ knit on RS, purl on WS
- ⊡ purl on RS, knit on WS
- ☑ s1 pwise wyif: slip 1 stitch purlwise with yarn at front of work
- ☑ s1 pwise wyib: slip 1 stitch purlwise with yarn at back of work
- ✳ insert right-hand needle under loose strands below and knit next stitch, catching in loose strands
- ——— slip next 6 stitches onto cable needle and wrap working yarn counterclockwise around them 4 times, k2, p2, k2 from cable needle

DIP AND ROW-BELOW STITCHES

All of these patterns involve dipping down into or catching up stitches from rows below the live one. Work these techniques carefully at first if you are new to them, being sure to pick up the correct stitch, or the pattern will not work out properly. Getting the tension right can take a bit of experimentation with some of the stitches, so work swatches before you start on projects.

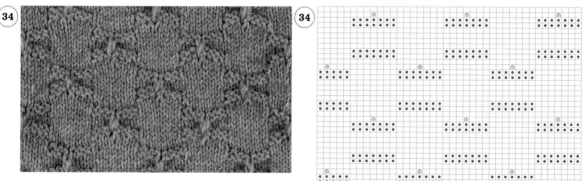

Key

- ☐ knit on RS, purl on WS
- ⊡ purl on RS, knit on WS
- ⌂ on WS knit into stitch on row below
- ⌂ on RS knit into stitch on row below

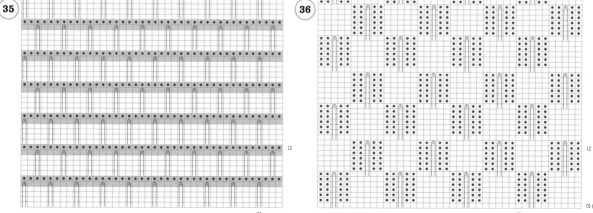

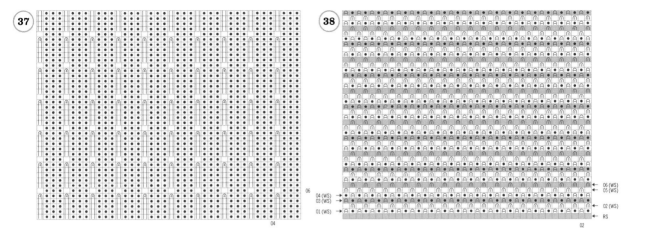

(37)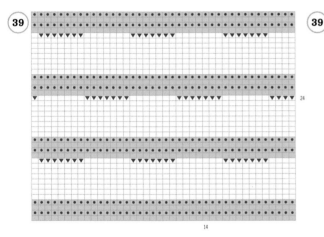

(38)

(39)

(39)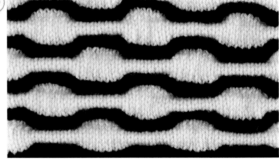

⊡ purl next stitch together with same stitch 7 rows below
from RS insert RH needle into stitch 6 rows below, pull up

⋔ long stitch, transfer it onto LH needle and knit it together
with next stitch
From RS insert RH needle into stitch 8 rows below, pull up

⋔ long stitch, transfer it onto LH needle and knit it together
with next stitch

⋔ tuck 4: drop 1st stitch off LH needle and use tip of RH
needle to unravel 4 rows, insert RH needle into live stitch
with horizontal strands on top of needle, knit live stitch,
catching in strands

⋔ tuck 5: drop 1st stitch off LH needle and use tip of RH
needle to unravel 5 rows, insert RH needle into live stitch
with horizontal strands on top of needle, knit live stitch,
catching in strands

⋔ tuck 6: drop 1st stitch off LH needle and use tip of RH
needle to unravel 6 rows, insert RH needle into live stitch
with horizontal strands on top of needle, knit live stitch,
catching in strands

(40)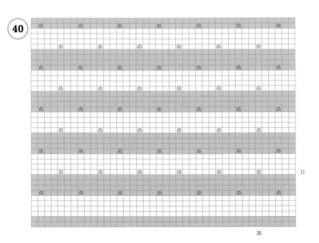

BOBBLES

Wonderfully perky, bobbles offer deep texture that works well for borders and edge patterning, as well as all-over designs. Do be aware that these patterns are yarn-hungry; bobbles are demanding that way. You can work your favourite bobble on these charts, so try different ones on swatches to see which size and shape you prefer.

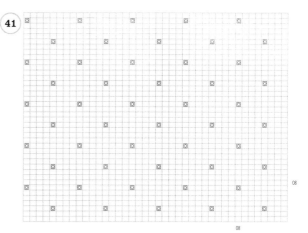

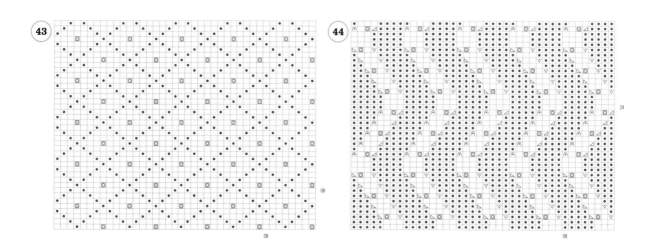

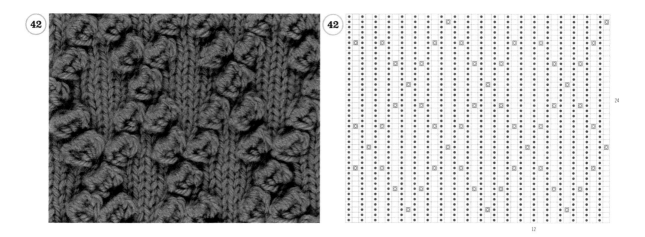

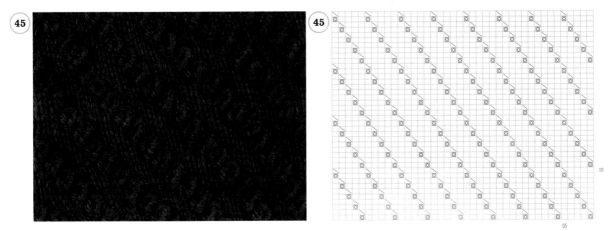

Key

- ☐ knit on RS, purl on WS
- ⊡ purl on RS, knit on WS
- ⊻ m1: make 1 stitch
- ○ bobble
- ◪ k2tog: knit 2 stitches together
- ◺ skpo: slip 1 stitch, knit 1 stitch, pass slipped stitch over
- ◸ knit through back loop (ktbl) on RS, purl through back loop (ptbl) on WS
- ▣ yf: yarn forward

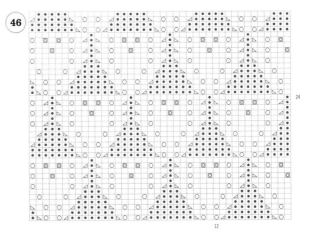

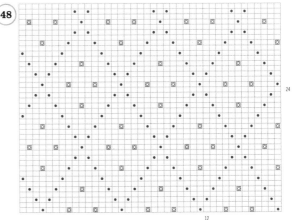

CABLES

Cables are one of those knitting techniques that many novice knitters avoid because they look so complicated and scary; but they really are easier than they look. You need a cable needle (two cable needles for a couple of these patterns), but the actual processes of forming the cables are really very simple (see page 246).

Key

- ☐ knit on RS, purl on WS
- ⊡ purl on RS, knit on WS
- ⟋⟍ slip next 2 stitches onto 1st cable needle and hold at back, slip next 2 stitches onto 2nd cable needle and hold at front, k2, p2 from 2nd cable needle, k2 from 1st cable needle
- ⟋⟍ C8Bp: slip next 4 stitches onto cable needle and hold at back, k1, p2, k1, then k1, p2, k1 from cable needle

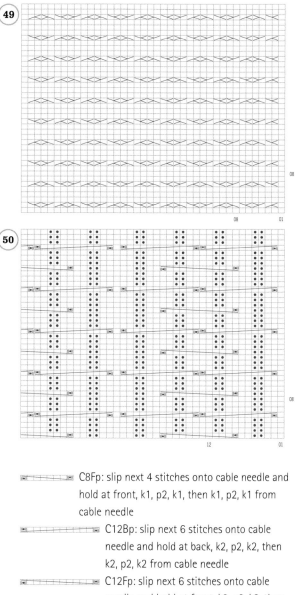

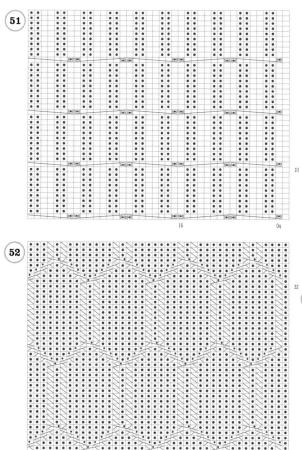

- ⟋⟍ C8Fp: slip next 4 stitches onto cable needle and hold at front, k1, p2, k1, then k1, p2, k1 from cable needle
- ⟋⟍ C12Bp: slip next 6 stitches onto cable needle and hold at back, k2, p2, k2, then k2, p2, k2 from cable needle
- ⟋⟍ C12Fp: slip next 6 stitches onto cable needle and hold at front, k2, p2, k2, then k2, p2, k2 from cable needle

53

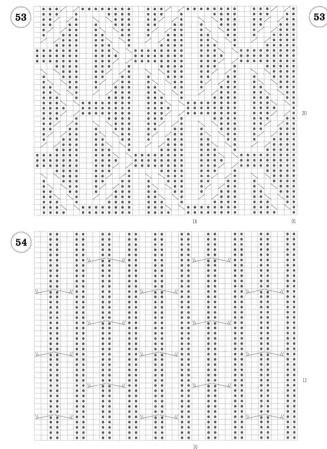

53

54

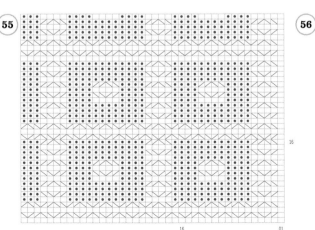

⚞⚟ C3B: slip next stitch onto cable needle and hold at back, k2, k1 from cable needle

⚞⚟ C3F: slip next stitch onto cable needle and hold at front, k2, k1 from cable needle

⚞⚟ C4B slip next 2 stitches onto cable needle and hold at back, k2, k2 from cable needle

⚞⚟ C4F: slip next 2 stitches onto cable needle and hold at front, k2, k2 from cable needle

⚞⚟ C2B: slip next stitch onto cable needle and hold at back, k1, k1 from cable needle

⚞⚟ C2F: slip next stitch onto cable needle and hold at front, k1, k1 from cable needle

⚞⚟ slip next stitch onto cable needle and hold at back, k1, p1tbl from cable needle

⚞⚟ slip next stitch onto cable needle and hold at front, p1tbl, k1 from cable needle

⚞⚟ slip next stitch onto 1st cable needle and hold at back, slip next stitch onto 2nd cable needle and hold at back, k1tbl, p1 from 2nd cable needle, k1tbl from 1st cable needle

⚞⚟ slip next stitch onto 1st cable needle and hold at front, slip next stitch onto 2nd cable needle and hold at back, k1tbl, p1 from 2nd cable needle, k1tbl from 1st cable needle

55

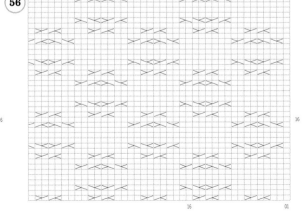

56

CABLES WITH TWIST STITCHES

These mini-cables don't need a cable needle to make them. Instead, the stitches are twisted by working them off the left-hand needle in the order given, rather than starting with the stitch nearest the tip of the needle. They can be a bit awkward at first, but once you pick up the technique, these are very satisfying patterns to work.

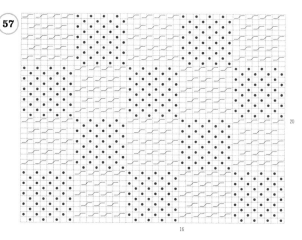

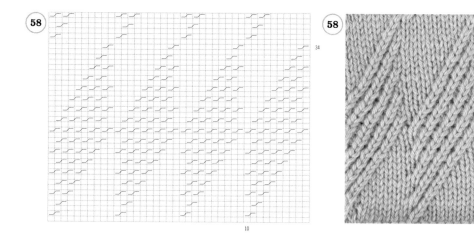

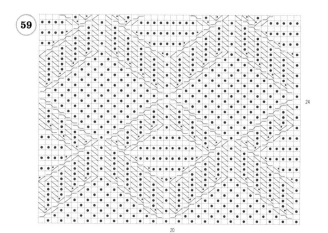

Key

▫ knit on RS, purl on WS

• purl on RS, knit on WS

⌐ T2R: k into front of 2nd stitch then k into back of 1st stitch then slip both sts off LH needle together

⌐ T2L: k into back of 2nd stitch then k into front of 1st stitch then slip both sts off LH needle together

⌐ T2Rp: on RS k into front of 2nd stitch then p into front of 1st stitch then slip both sts off LH needle together: on WS k into front of 2nd stitch then p into front of 1st stitch then slip both stitches off LH needle together

⌐ T2Lp: on RS and on WS p into back of 2nd stitch then k into front of 1st stitch then slip both sts off LH needle together

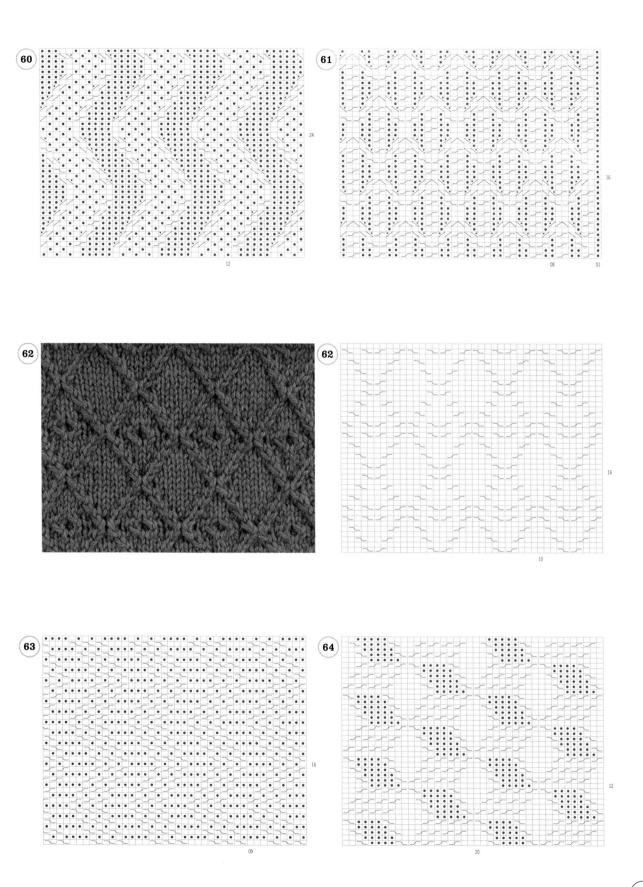

SHORT-REPEAT LACE

These are lace patterns with repeats of 10 stitches or fewer. They are a great starting point if you are new to lace knitting. Some people prefer to write the repeat out and work from that, as the charts can look a bit complicated until you get used to them.

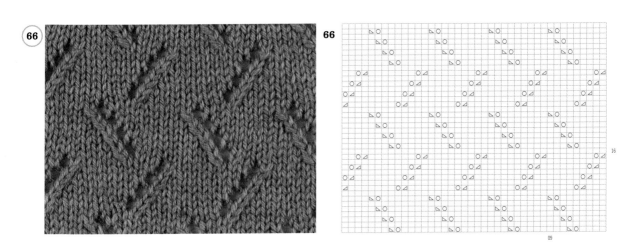

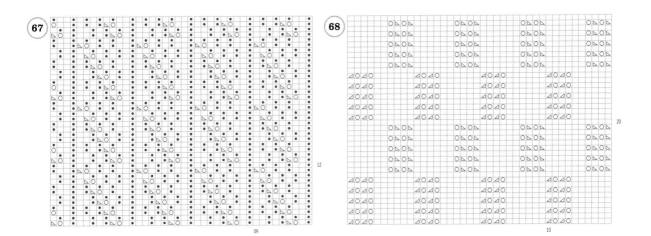

69

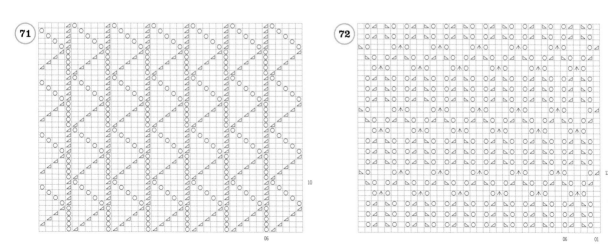

69

70

Key

☐ knit on RS, purl on WS

⊡ purl on RS, knit on WS

◿ k2tog: knit 2 stitches together

◺ skpo: slip 1 stitch, knit 1 stitch, pass slipped stitch over

⊙ yf: yarn forward

⩚ s2kpo: slip 2 stitches together, knit 1 stitch, pass slipped stitches over

◿ knit through back loop (ktbl) on RS, purl through back loop (ptbl) on WS

71

72

LONGER-REPEAT LACE

These lace patterns have repeats of more than 10 stitches and create beautifully intricate knitted fabrics. Lace knitting is something that many knitters find addictive, and working some of the very complex patterns can be both challenging and satisfying. Nothing here is going to drive you crazy, however.

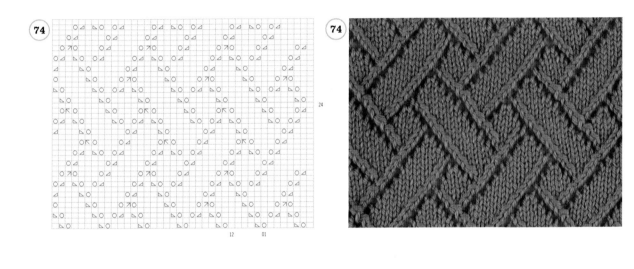

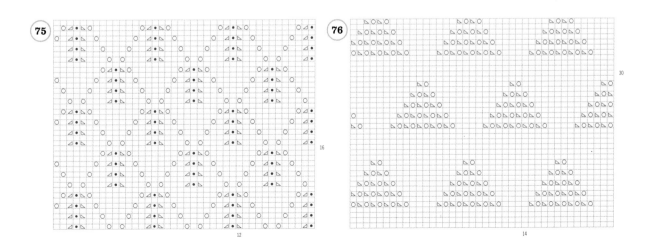

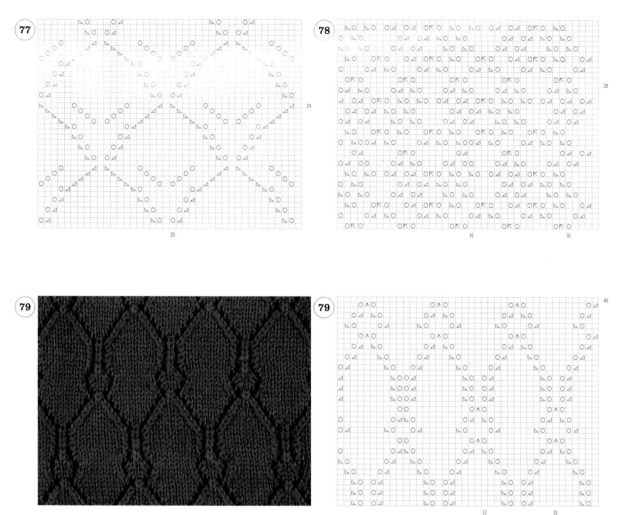

Key
- ☐ knit on RS, purl on WS
- • purl on RS, knit on WS
- ◿ k2tog: knit 2 stitches together
- ◹ skpo: slip 1 stitch, knit 1 stitch, pass slipped stitch over
- ○ yf: yarn forward
- ⧄ s2kpo: slip 2 stitches together, knit 1 stitch, pass slipped stitches over

PINTUCKED SOCKS

Slouchy by design, these socks look great with sneakers or clogs, or even with high-heeled pumps. The tucks are knitted in to the cuffs, and using a variegated yarn gives you colour patterning without the need to ever change yarns.

YARNS

Rowan Fine Art: 1 × 100g (437 yds) hank in Maple (310)

TOOLS

Set of 2.5mm (US 2) double-pointed knitting needles
Stitch markers
Stitch holders
Blunt tapestry needle

TENSION

32 sts and 42 rows to 10cm (4in) using 2.5mm (US 2) 2.5mm needles and measured over st st

MEASUREMENTS

One size fits adult shoe size 5–7 (7–9)

ABBREVIATIONS

See page 252

SOCK

(make 2 alike)

Cast on 64 sts and join in the round, taking care not to twist the cast-on edge; place a marker.

Round 1 (RS): [K1tbl, p1] to end of round.

Rep round 1, 16 more times.

Knit 9 rounds.

Commence pattern repeat

Round 1: *K4, [use RH needle to pick up purl bump of the next st 7 rows below the next st on the LH needle and place on the LH needle making sure it is not twisted, knit this picked up st and the next st on the LH needle tog] 4 times; rep from * to end.

Rounds 2–8: Knit.

Round 9: *[Pick up a purl bump as before and k2tog as before] 4 times, k4; rep from * to end of round.

Rounds 10–16: Knit.

These 16 rounds set the pattern. Repeat twice more.

Knit 8 rounds.

Shape heel

Row 1 (RS): Knit first 16 sts to be used for the heel.

Slip next 32 sts onto a stitch holder, to be used later for the foot. (32 sts)

Row 2: P across 16 sts from first and fourth needles, to last st, wrap next st (slip next st from left needle onto right needle, taking yarn to opposite side of the work between needles and then slip same st back onto left needle – when working back across wrapped sts, i.e., from Row 23, work the wrapped st and the wrapping loop(s) tog as one st) and turn.

Row 3: K to last st, wrap next st and turn.

Row 4: P to last 2 sts, wrap next st and turn.

Row 5: K to last 2 sts, wrap next st and turn.

Row 6: P to last 3 sts, wrap next st and turn.

Row 7: K to last 3 sts, wrap next st and turn.

Row 8: P to last 4 sts, wrap next st and turn.

Row 9: K to last 4 sts, wrap next st and turn.

Row 10: P to last 5 sts, wrap next st and turn.

Row 11: K to last 5 sts, wrap next st and turn.

Row 12: P to last 6 sts, wrap next st and turn.

Row 13: K to last 6 sts, wrap next st and turn.

Row 14: P to last 7 sts, wrap next st and turn.

Row 15: K to last 7 sts, wrap next st and turn.

Row 16: P to last 8 sts, wrap next st and turn.

Row 17: K to last 8 sts, wrap next st and turn.

Row 18: P to last 9 sts, wrap next st and turn.

Row 19: K to last 9 sts, wrap next st and turn.

Row 20: P to last 10 sts, wrap next st and turn.

Row 21: K to last 10 sts, wrap next st and turn.

Rows 22–23: as rows 18–19.

Rows 24–25: as rows 16–17.

Rows 26 and 27: as rows 14–15.

Rows 28–29: as rows 12–13.

Rows 30–31: as rows 10–11.

Rows 32–33: as rows 8–9.

Rows 34–35: as rows 6–7.

Rows 36–37: as rows 4–5.

Rows 38–39: as rows 2–3.

Row 40: P to end.

This is now the start of each new round; place a marker.

Slip 32 sts from holder back onto needles and recommence working in the round until work measures 21cm (8¼in) from back of heel.

Place markers before the first st and after the 32nd st.

Shape toe

Round 1: [K2 skpo, k to 4 sts before marker, k2tog, k2, slip marker] twice.

Round 2: Knit.

Repeat last 2 rounds, 7 more times. (32 sts).

Redistribute sts so that there are 16 sts on two needles.

Turn sock inside out and bind (cast) off using the 3-needle method.

(Stitches can be grafted if preferred to close the toe).

FINISHING

Weave in any loose end and press according to ball band instructions.

WRAPPING AND TURNING STITCHES

On a knit side row:

Keeping the yarn in back, slip the next stitch purlwise from the left needle to the right needle. Bring the yarn forward as if to purl. Slip the stitch from the right needle back to the left needle. Turn the work so the purl side is facing you, ready to purl.

On a purl side row:

Keeping the yarn in front, slip the next stitch purlwise from the left needle to the right needle. Bring the yarn back as if to knit. Slip the stitch from the right needle back to the left needle. Bring the yarn to the front of the work as if to purl. Turn the work so the knit side is facing you, ready to knit.

9

COMBINING PATTERNS

This chapter is an exercise in developing your own creative ideas. I have made suggestions for taking those ideas a stage further by combining one or more of the charts within this book, but you should be guided by your own personal taste. Whatever you decide, don't be afraid to make things your own.

COMBINATIONS

I've used complementary colours for the charts in this chapter, but why not clash everything together in a riot of pinks and orange? Add beads and embroidery or leave things bare – the choice is yours!

▲ This swatch has a funky retro feel to it. The stripes and ovals, especially in the monochrome palette, would not have been out of place on the walls of a 1960s boutique. This would look fabulous as a throw for a chair or a couch. Add silver beads on some of the vertical stripes for additional shimmer.

◀ *In this chart, I have combined two of the textured stitches from Chapter 7 and added some edge stitches to prevent the edges curling. If you are using a DK weight yarn, this swatch size is ideal width for a snood. Just continue with the repeat as set or add some of the other texture stitches in the book. Work until the piece reaches 105cm (42in) and then cast off. Sew the short ends together for a snood you can wear long or loop twice around your neck.*

▼ *This swatch has a Turkish feel with the strong diamond motif. The combination of large and small diamonds adds interest, and beads or embroidery (see page 249) in an accent colour to the large diamonds would make this extra special. Either work the border and main piece as one or knit the border separately and join with a slip stitch afterwards.*

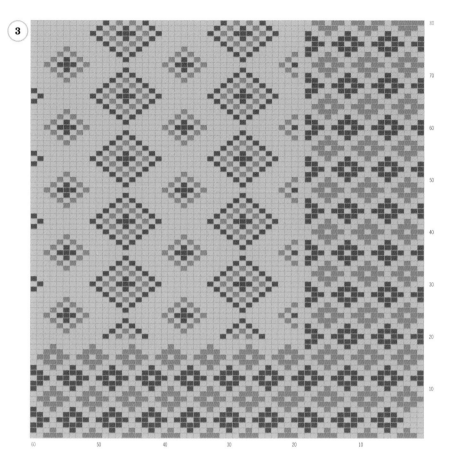

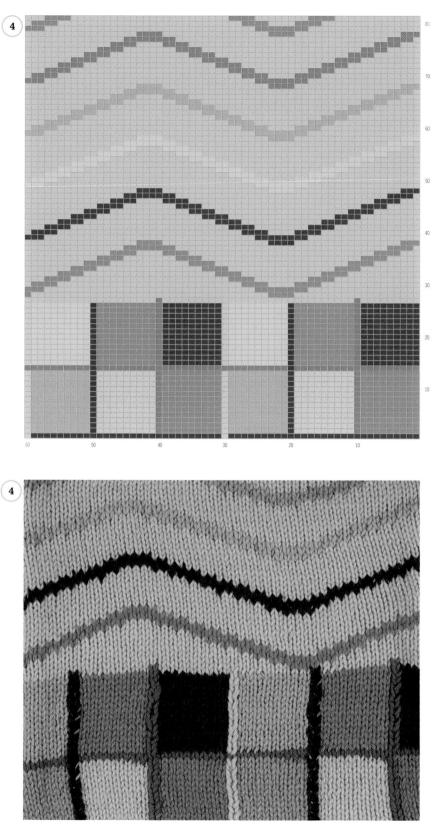

◄ This is a fun, colourful piece that has the potential to have more added. For instance, some of the vertical lines of the plaid could be worked in Swiss darning (see page 241) with either an opaque or metallic yarn. Some of the horizontal chevrons could be beaded or embroidered (see page 249). If you prefer muted colours, try a combination of creams, caramels and chocolates for a rather more understated result.

ROSE AND GINGHAM TABLE RUNNER

This pretty Rose and Gingham Table Runner will make a stylish centrepiece to any table. I have combined both check and floral patterns in this design and suggest using the stranding technique (see page 239) to knit the checks while working bobbins of yarn for the central floral motif. Leave nice loose strands across the back of the gingham check to prevent pulling and to ensure a nice even look at the front of the work.

YARNS
Rowan Pure Wool Worsted
1 × 100g (219 yds) balls each in shades: Periwinkle, Ocean, Navy, Ivory, and Splash

TOOLS
4.75mm (US 7) needles
Tapestry needle for sewing in ends

TENSION
20 sts × 25 rows over 10cm (4in) using 4.75mm (US 7) needles measured over st st

MEASUREMENTS
23cm wide × 56cm long (9in wide × 22in long)

TABLE RUNNER
Using 4.75mm (US 7) needles and Periwinkle, CO 50 sts
Work 4 rows in garter stitch.
Begin working from chart remembering to work the 3 garter stitches at each end of every row.
Increase 2 stitches across Row 20 as shown in the chart (52 sts).
Keep working the chart until you have worked the rose pattern a total of 4 times ending on Row 38 of the rose chart.
Next: Work the gingham check and, using Ivory for the centre motif, work 3 rows in stocking stitch decreasing 2 stitches across the third row as follows: pattern 18 sts, k2tog, pattern 13 sts, k2tog, pattern to the end. (50 sts)
Next: Work the check pattern as set, using Ivory, knit the next row and break the Ivory yarn leaving a tail for sewing in later, work check pattern to the end of the row. Continue working in gingham pattern still working the 3 garter stitches at each outer edge, as set at the beginning of the chart, for a further 18 rows.
Change to periwinkle and work four rows garter stitch.
Cast off.

FINISHING
Weave in all the loose yarn ends.
Wet block the whole runner (see page 251). When dry, you could also steam the piece gently for a sharper finish.

Key
- ☐ Ivory
- ☐ RS: Knit WS: Purl
- ☐ Navy
- ☐ Ocean
- ☐ Periwinkle
- ☐ Splash
- ☐ Grey no stitch
- ☐ RS: Purl WS: Knit
- ☐ RS: Purl into fb WS: Knit into fb

10

TECHNIQUES

Although it's tucked away at the end of the book, this chapter is one of the most important. Colourwork requires mastering quite a few technical knitting skills. Here I will explain how those skills work and the easiest ways to achieve them, plus I've included a handy guide to finishing and embellishing your work.

COLOUR TECHNIQUES

Many knitters avoid colourwork as they think it is too complicated. It does take practice, true, but here I will guide you through all the basic steps to get started. Take your time and, with only a little practice, you'll soon be a devotee of these techniques.

INTARSIA

Many of the charts in this book require you to work the intarsia technique. The most important thing to get right is the way the yarns link at the colour changes to prevent holes from appearing in your knitting, and while the principle of doing this is always the same, it does vary in its detail depending on the outline shape you are knitting. So if you are an intarsia novice, practise the variations carefully on a swatch to get the best results.

YARN BOBBINS

If you are knitting a motif with several colours, you need to have a separate yarn supply for each one, so you will need to make up little bobbins of yarn. You can buy plastic bobbins to wind yarn around, or make these yarn butterfly bobbins.

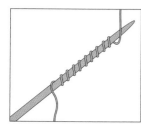

1 To establish how much yarn you need for part of a motif, count roughly how many stitches it contains: let's say there are 70. Loosely wind the yarn around a knitting needle 10 times, then measure out seven times the wound length. Add a bit extra for safety and for sewing in the ends (see page 250), and that's your bobbin quantity.

2 Lay the tail end of the yarn in the middle of your palm, then wrap the length of yarn in a figure of eight around your thumb and little finger.

3 Take the butterfly bobbin off your fingers and wind the tail that was in the middle of your palm tightly around the middle and tuck the end under the wraps. Pull gently on the loose end to pull out the yarn from the centre of the bobbin.

JOINING IN A NEW COLOUR YARN

This is the method for joining in a new colour in the middle of a row. Twisting the yarns in this way will help to tension the first new colour stitch correctly and prevent it from twisting.

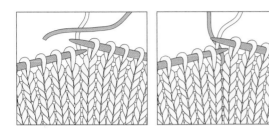

1 *At the change in colour on a knit row, lay the new colour yarn over the old colour yarn, as shown.*

2 *Twist the new colour under the old colour, bringing it around into the right position to knit with.*

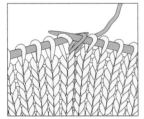

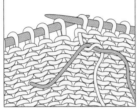

3 *Knit the first stitch in the new colour. At the end of the row, pull gently on the tail of yarn to tighten the first stitch. When the knitting is complete, weave in the loose tails (see page 250).*

4 *At the change in colour on a purl row, lay the new colour yarn over the old colour yarn and make one complete twist, as shown.*

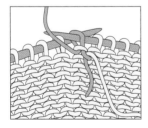

5 *Purl the first stitch in the new colour. Tighten stitches and weave in ends as for a knit row.*

CHANGING COLOUR IN A STRAIGHT VERTICAL LINE

Try to work in an even tension across the colour change, rather than pulling the first stitch in the new colour as tight as possible. Doing that will just distort the last stitch in that colour on the previous row. You can adjust baggy stitches once the knitting is complete.

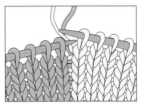

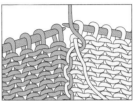

1 *At the change in colour on a knit row, bring the new colour under the old colour and up into position to knit with. Drop the old colour and knit with the new colour.*

2 *On a purl row, bring the new colour under and around the old colour from left to right, as shown. Drop the old colour and purl with the new colour.*

CHANGING COLOUR ON A RIGHT-SLOPING DIAGONAL

Because the colour change is moving on each row, the yarns are linked in a slightly different way to a straight line colour change (see above). Note that the diagonal will slope to the left on the wrong side of the knitting.

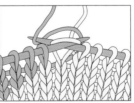

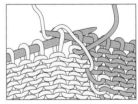

1 *At the change in colour on a knit row, bring the new colour under the old colour and up, ready to knit with. Drop the old colour and knit with the new colour.*

2 *On a purl row, bring the new colour across and purl with it: you are not actually interlinking the yarns, but as the colours are moving across by one stitch, a hole won't form.*

CHANGING COLOUR ON A LEFT-SLOPING DIAGONAL

Note that the diagonal will slope to the right on the wrong side of the knitting.

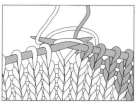 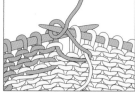

1 At the change in colour on a knit row, bring the new colour under the old colour and up ready to knit with. Drop the old colour and knit with the new colour.

2 On a purl row, bring the new colour under the old colour and around ready to purl with. Drop the old colour and purl with the new colour.

CARRYING A COLOUR ACROSS THE BACK OF THE KNITTING

Here is how to carry a colour farther along a row from where it was last used, so that it is in the right position on the next row. Alternatively, you can strand the yarn to the right position on the previous row.

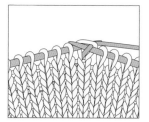 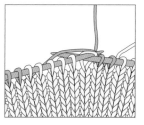 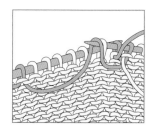

1 On a knit row, bring the new colour yarn across the back of the knitting to where it is needed. Keep the strand of yarn quite loose. Knit the first stitch needed in the new colour.

2 You need to catch in the loose strand as you knit across the row. This is done the same way on a purl row and you may find those illustrations clearer (see steps 3–5). Put the tip of the right-hand needle knitwise into the next stitch and then under the loose strand. Knit with the new colour, but do not let the loose strand come through with the new stitch. Repeat on every alternate stitch to catch all of the strand against the back of the knitting.

3 On a purl row, bring the new colour across to where it is needed. Keep the strand of yarn quite loose and take it under the old colour, then purl the first stitch needed in the new colour.

4 To catch in the loose strand, put the tip of the right-hand needle purlwise into the next stitch and then under the loose strand.

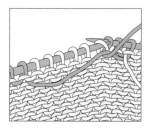

5 Purl with the new colour, not allowing the strand to come through with the new stitch. Repeat on every alternate stitch to catch all of the strand against the back of the knitting.

STRANDING

You may be familiar with the term 'Fair Isle' for this method of colour knitting, but strictly speaking Fair Isle is a type of stranded knitting. The two most popular ways to work this type of knitting involve either working with one yarn at a time and dropping the yarn not in use, or working holding a yarn in each hand. Once mastered, the latter is the quickest and can produce very even results. Both techniques are shown here, so experiment to see which suits you best. A very important thing to get right is the tension on the floats – the strands of yarn lying across the back of the knitting. If they are too tight, then the knitting will be puckered, too loose, and the stitches will be baggy. If you spread out the stitches on the right-hand needle before you change colour, then bring the new colour across the back and work the first stitch with it, the tension should be right. As you become more familiar with the technique, you'll get better at judging this tension. As with intarsia knitting (see page 236), try to work in an even tension across the colour change, rather than pulling the first stitch in the new colour as tight as possible. You can adjust baggy stitches once the knitting is complete.

WORKING WITH ONE YARN AT A TIME

This is the simplest way of stranding and one to try if you are a beginner to colour knitting, but it is the slowest method.

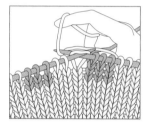 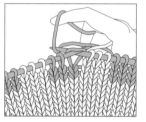 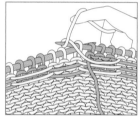 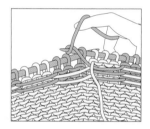

1 *At the colour change on a knit row, drop the old colour and pick up the new colour, bringing it across the back and over the old colour. Knit with the new colour.*

2 *At the next colour change, repeat the process, but bring the new colour across and under the old colour. Taking the yarns over and under one another in this systematic way will make them interlace neatly on the back.*

3 *The principle is the same on a purl row. At one colour change, bring the new yarn over the old yarn.*

4 *At the next colour change, bring the new yarn under the old yarn.*

WORKING WITH ONE YARN IN EACH HAND

Most people have one dominant hand and will find it difficult to control the yarn with the other hand, but practice will help. Hold the yarn that appears more often – or first – in your dominant hand and that which appears less often – or second – in your other hand.

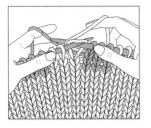 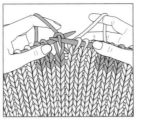  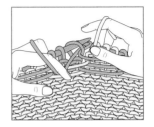

1 *On a knit row, knit the stitches in the first colour.*

2 *When the second colour yarn is needed, work with the other hand. Holding the yarns like this means that the colours will automatically interlace neatly on the back.*

3 *The principle is exactly the same on a purl row, though you may have to adjust the position of your fingers to catch the yarn with the needle. Purl the first colour, controlling the yarn with one hand.*

4 *Purl the second colour with the other hand.*

CATCHING IN FLOATS

If there are five or more stitches between different colours, then you need to trap the floats against the back of the knitting to prevent long floats catching and to help tension the stitches neatly. The simple way of doing this is to use the working yarn to trap the float against the back of every second or third stitch.

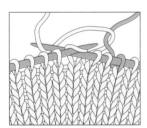 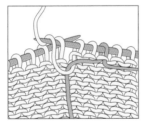

1 *On a knit row, insert the right-hand needle into the stitch. Lay the yarn to be trapped over the working yarn, then knit the stitch. Make sure the trapped yarn does not appear through the stitch; it should just be held firmly against the back of it.*

2 *On a purl row, insert the right-hand needle into the stitch. Lay the yarn to be trapped in over the working yarn, then purl the stitch.*

WEAVING IN FLOATS

If you hold yarns in both hands for stranded knitting, hold them the same way to weave the floats into the back. This is a good idea on garments and blankets, because fingers can snag loosely caught floats. If you are weaving in across the same stitches for several rows, don't weave in to the back of the same stitch each time as this will create a ridge that shows on the front. Hold the yarn you are knitting with in your dominant hand and the yarn to be woven in with the other.

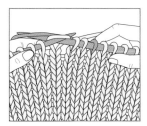 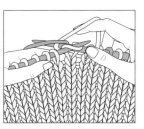

1 *On a knit row, insert the right-hand needle into the stitch. Lay the yarn to be woven in over the needle's tip.*

2 *Wrap the working yarn around the tip of the needle ready to knit it.*

SWISS DARNING

This is an embroidery stitch specific to knitting. It matches the stitches on the right side of stocking stitch and is sometimes called 'duplicate stitch'. Swiss darning can be used to work whole areas of a motif, decorate designs or correct mistakes. Use yarn that is the same weight as that used to knit with for the best effect.

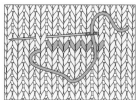 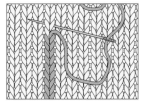 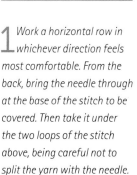

1 *Work a horizontal row in whichever direction feels most comfortable. From the back, bring the needle through at the base of the stitch to be covered. Then take it under the two loops of the stitch above, being careful not to split the yarn with the needle.*

2 *Pull the yarn through so that it lies flat over one 'leg' of the stitch. Take the needle back through the base – where it came out – and pull the yarn through so it lies neatly over the knitted stitch. Bring the needle to the front again through the base of the next stitch.*

3 *To work a vertical row, bring the needle through the base of the stitch to be covered and take it under the loops of the stitch above. Take the needle back through the base of the stitch. Bring it to the front again through the base of the stitch above.*

SLIP STITCH TECHNIQUES

Above and beyond knitting and purling, the only technique required for slip stitch knitting is, as the name suggests, slipping stitches. This means just passing them from the left-hand needle to the right-hand needle without knitting or purling them. You'll usually only need to slip stitches purlwise, whether it's a knit or a purl row, so that the stitch isn't twisted. However, there are a few variations that some patterns will ask for.

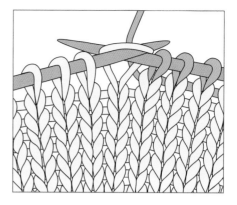

SLIPPING KNITWISE ON A KNIT ROW

Sometimes you may need to slip a stitch knitwise on a knit row in order to twist it.

Insert the right-hand needle from left to right into the front of the next stitch on the left-hand needle, as if you were going to knit it, and just slip it onto the right-hand needle.

A stitch can be slipped knitwise on a purl row in the same way: just insert the needle into the front of the stitch from left to right.

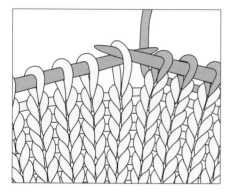

SLIPPING PURLWISE ON A KNIT ROW

This is how to slip a stitch purlwise on a knit row.

Insert the right-hand needle from right to left into the front of the next stitch on the left-hand needle, and then just slip it onto the right-hand needle.

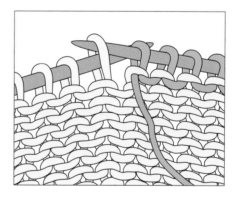

SLIPPING PURLWISE ON A PURL ROW

This is how to slip a stitch purlwise on a purl row.

Insert the right-hand needle from right to left into the front of the next stitch on the left-hand needle, as if you were going to purl it, and just slip it onto the right-hand needle.

SLIPPING A STITCH WITH YARN IN FRONT

Some slip stitch patterns – usually texture patterns – will ask you to take the yarn to the front when slipping a stitch on a knit row (see also Knitting Notes).

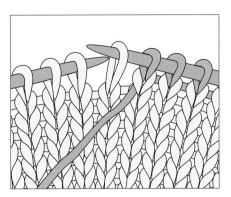

On a knit row the working yarn will naturally be on the side facing away from you, at the back of the knitting. Bring the yarn between the tips of the needles to the front of the knitting, then slip the stitch as instructed (here it has been slipped purlwise), then take the yarn between the needles to the back of the work again, ready to knit the next stitch. This leaves a little bar of yarn in front of the slipped stitch on the right side of the knitting.

SLIPPING A STITCH WITH YARN IN BACK

Some patterns will ask you to take the yarn to the back when slipping a stitch on a purl row (see also Knitting Notes).

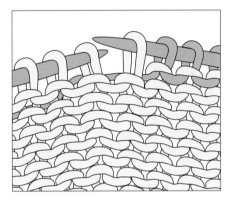

On a purl row the working yarn will naturally be on the side facing towards you, at the front of the knitting. Take the yarn between the tips of the needles to the back of the knitting, then slip the stitch as instructed (here it has been slipped purlwise), then take the yarn between the needles to the front of the work again, ready to purl the next stitch. This leaves a little bar of yarn in front of the slipped stitch on the right side of the knitting.

Knitting Notes

The instructions for taking yarn back or forward before slipping stitches can be written in two ways. Some patterns will say, 'k1, yf, sl 1, yb, k1'. So you will knit one stitch, bring the yarn forward, slip one stitch, take the yarn back, knit one stitch. This can also be written as, 'k1, sl 1 wyif, k1', with 'wyif' the abbreviation for 'with yarn in front'. Similarly, on a purl row the instruction can be written as 'p1, yb, sl1, yf, p1', or as 'p1, sl 1 wyib, p1', with 'wyib', the abbreviation for 'with yarn in back'.

MOSAIC PATTERNS

This type of pattern is probably what many people envisage when they think of slip stitch knitting. Celebrated knitter Barbara G. Walker was a big fan of slip stitch mosaics – indeed, she coined that name for them – and her enthusiasm did a lot to popularise the patterns. You can form quite complicated patterns using just one colour of yarn at a time, although the repeats can be quite long so you have to pay attention to the first of each pair of rows, but then you just copy the pattern when working back across for the second row. As you have to effectively knit each row twice, the knitting is quite slow to grow.

1 Mosaic patterns are often shown worked in stocking stitch, and in many ways this is the easiest stitch to use as the yarn is naturally always on the right side of the work when you slip the stitches. The pattern shows clearly on the flat fabric and you just need to accept that the longer slipped stitches are intrinsic to the technique, even if you're a beginner knitter and have only just managed to achieve an even tension on ordinary stocking stitch.

2 Mosaic patterns are also very successful knitted in garter stitch. The longer slipped stitches blend into the textured surface better than they do in flat stocking stitch. Although the texture does also blur the pattern a bit, stick to strongly contrasting colours and the results will be fine (see also swatch 5). When knitting the wrong-side rows, you do need to bring the yarn forward before slipping the stitches to prevent a bar appearing on the right side.

3 A third option is to use a combination of garter and stocking stitch, and this can have an excellent effect. You can choose either colour for either stitch: in this swatch the lines are in garter and the background in stocking stitch. The textured lines are slightly proud of the flat background, emphasising the patterning even further.

4 When working stocking stitch mosaics you can choose less contrasting colours and still have the patterns work well. These two shades of green are harmonious for an overall quite subtle effect, but using the darker value colour for the lines keeps the pattern clear enough.

5 *However, the same palette and pattern worked in garter stitch effectively shows how the texture of the stitch pattern blurs the design. The horizontal garter ridges confuse the eye and the darker lines are much harder to see as shapes than they are in swatch 4. If you're planning a mosaic project, do try swatching your chosen colours in all the stitch combinations as the pattern can look quite different in each.*

6 *Even in flat stocking stitch you will struggle to make colours of a similar value work well in a mosaic design. Photographed in black and white it would be impossible to discern a difference between the green and brown in this swatch, and it's almost as hard to see the pattern in the colour version.*

7 *Choice of yarn can make a big difference in mosaic knitting. Lightweight mercerised cotton yarn will highlight (in the worst way) every elongated stitch and will wriggle and twist very obviously if your tension is anything short of perfect. A good choice is a wool/man-made fibre mix that has reasonable elasticity and a matte finish, and if it is loosely plied, like the yarn used in this swatch, so much the better. While this yarn might not be the simplest to knit with (it's a bit too easy to split the yarn with your needle while forming a stitch), the loose twist means that it fills out the stitch a bit, making the inevitable small gaps less obvious.*

CABLES AND LACE

These are two very different techniques, but both can add dramatically to the look of your knitting. The cable, which looks like twisted rope, is a technique where, with the help of a cable needle, you knit your stitches in a different order from how they appear on the needle, thus creating a twist. Lace, on the other hand, is merely a series of decorative increases and decreases.

CABLE

Projects can be cabled to add an extra dimension to a knitted piece. Work a test before starting a project, as the results can vary depending on the width and length of the cable. Shown here is a cable six back (C6B) and cable six front (C6F), though almost any number of stitches can be cabled.

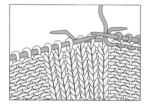

1 *For a cable six back, work to the position of the cable. Slip the next three stitches from the left-hand needle onto the cable needle. Leave this at the back of the knitting.*

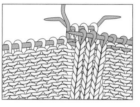

2 *Knit the next three stitches from the left-hand needle.*

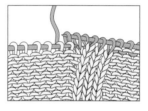

3 *Knit the three stitches that are held on the cable needle to complete the cable six back: the twist will go to the right.*

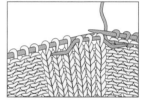

4 *For a cable six front, work to the position of the cable. Slip the next three stitches from the left-hand needle onto the cable needle. Leave this at the front of the knitting.*

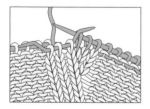

5 *Knit the next three stitches from the left-hand needle.*

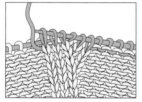

6 *Knit the three stitches that are held on the cable needle to complete the cable six front: the twist will go to the left.*

LACE

Lace knitting, although complex in appearance, is really only a pattern made of holes. The holes are achieved by making a stitch with a 'yarn forward'. However, it follows that if you are making a stitch in this way, you will then have too many on the needle by the end of the row. Therefore, after every 'yarn forward' instruction there will follow an instruction to make a decrease.

YARN FORWARD (YF):
This is how to work a yarn forward between two knit stitches.

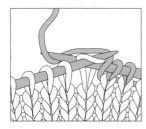 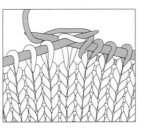

1 Bring the yarn forward between the tips of the needles.

2 Take the yarn over the right-hand needle to the back of the knitting and knit the next stitch.

SLIP ONE, KNIT ONE, PASS THE SLIPPED STITCH OVER (SKPO):
This decrease slants to the left on stocking stitch.

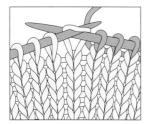 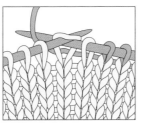 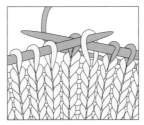

1 Slip the first stitch of the decrease knitwise onto the right-hand needle.

2 Knit the next stitch, the second one of the decrease stitches.

3 Without stretching the slipped stitch, put the tip of the left-hand needle into the front of it and lift it over the stitch just knitted and drop it off the needle.

SLIP, SLIP, KNIT (SSK):

This decrease slants to the left on stocking stitch and is neat and flat.

KNIT TWO STITCHES TOGETHER (K2TOG):

This decrease slants to the right in stocking stitch.

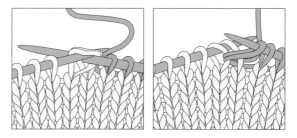

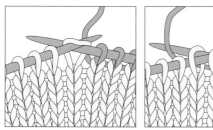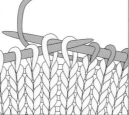

1 One at a time, slip the first and then the second of the decrease stitches knitwise onto the right-hand needle.

2 From the left, insert the left-hand needle into the fronts of these stitches and then knit them together. You are effectively knitting the slipped stitches together through the back loops, but having twisted them first.

1 From left to right, insert the right-hand needle through both decrease stitches.

2 Knit the two stitches together as if they were one.

PURL TWO STITCHES TOGETHER (P2TOG):

Used on a purl row, this decrease slants to the right on stocking stitch.

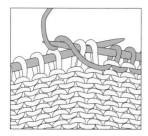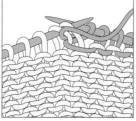

1 Insert the right-hand needle purlwise through both of the decrease stitches.

2 Purl the two stitches together as one.

BEADING

You can either completely bead a large area of knitting, or use beads, or sequins, to decorate a particular feature of a project. The technique you choose will depend on where you want to place beads. The beads need to suit the yarn – they can't be too heavy or they will stretch the stitches, and they can't be wider or longer than a knitted stitch or they will distort it.

THREADING BEADS ONTO YARN

The hole in the bead (or sequin) must be large enough for doubled yarn to pass through.

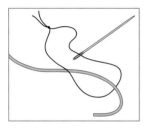

1 *Thread a sewing needle with a short length of sewing cotton and knot the ends. Put the tail end of the yarn through the loop of cotton and adjust the position of the knot so that it is clear of both the yarn and the needle (that way the bead* does not have to fit over the doubled yarn and the knot at the same time).

2 *Slip the beads onto the needle, down the thread and onto the yarn. Push the beads along the yarn as you work.*

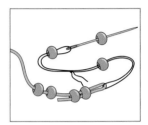

SLIP STITCH BEADING

This is an easy technique to work, but beads can only be placed on every alternate stitch and row, though those can be either knit or purl rows.

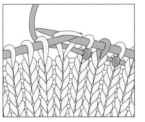

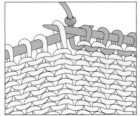

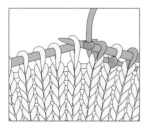

1 *On a knit row, work to the position of the bead. Bring the yarn forward between the needles, then slide a bead down the yarn so it sits right against the knitting. Slip the next stitch purlwise.*

2 *Take the yarn back between the needles, making sure the bead stays at the front. Knit the next stitch firmly. The bead is lying on a strand of yarn running across the base of the slipped stitch.*

3 *On a purl row, work to the position of the bead. Take the yarn back between the needles, slide a bead down against the knitting, and slip the next stitch purlwise. Purl the next stitch firmly.*

SLIP STITCH SEQUINS

The technique is shown here on a knit row, and the same principles apply on a purl row. Purling after the slipped stitch helps prevent the edge of the sequin from tucking into the knitting.

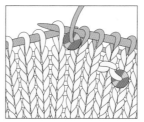

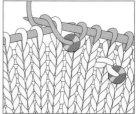

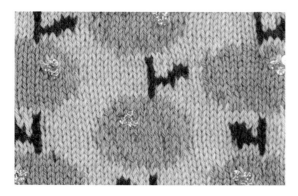

1 *Knit to the position of the sequin. Bring the yarn forward between the needles, then slide a sequin down the yarn so it sits right against the knitting. Slip the next stitch purlwise.*

2 *Purl the next stitch, then take the yarn back between the needles to continue knitting.*

FINISHING

After investing so much time, effort and love into knitting a piece of colourwork, I urge you to take the time to finish it properly. It really is worth going the extra mile because doing so will give your work a professional appearance.

WEAVING IN ENDS

Weave in the loose tails to secure them and stop the knitting from ever unravelling. The same method can be used for stripes, intarsia and stranded knitting. Always weave ends into the bumps of stitches in the same colour to prevent colours appearing in the wrong places on the right side of the knitting.

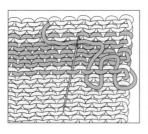

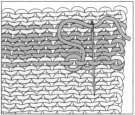

1 *Thread a blunt-tipped knitter's sewing needle or a tapestry needle with a tail of yarn. On the back of the knitting, take the needle in and out of three or four stitch bumps of the same colour. Here, the loops are shown loose for clarity, but you should pull the yarn gently taut as you go.*

2 *Work back along the bumps in the same way, but taking the yarn in the opposite direction to form loops, as shown. Cut the end short.*

DISGUISING MISTAKES

If you realise you have worked a stitch in the wrong colour several rows back and can't bear to unravel, then you can fix it later. Swiss darning (see page 241) can be used to hide any small (and sometimes quite large) mistakes in a knitted colour pattern. You can also use this stitch to work single stitches, or indeed to work large areas of a pattern, as in many charts in this book.

WET BLOCKING AND STEAMING

For best results I suggest wet blocking the swatches from this book. In order to do this, first thoroughly soak your piece of work in cool water. I add a small amount of wool conditioner to the water and leave for about 15 minutes. The soaking time allows the water to plump up the fibres and fill out the stitches.

Gently squeeze out the excess water. Do not wring. Wrap the swatch in a towel and roll up. Blot the excess water further until just damp. Using a flat surface or blocking board, pin the swatch into shape and leave to dry thoroughly.

If you are pressed for time, you can also block your swatch by using a steam iron. Adjust the iron to steam and hold it close above the swatch but not actually touching it. Allow the steam to relax the fibres and moisten the swatch. Pin into shape and allow to dry.

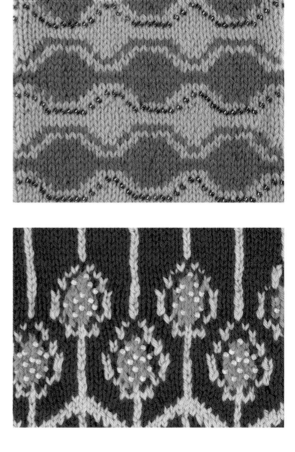

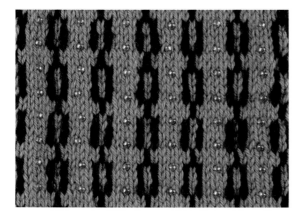

ABBREVIATIONS:

cm	centimetres
cn	cable needle
CO	cast on
cont	continue
dec	decrease
DK	double knit
dpns	double pointed needles
fb	increase by working into front and back of same stitch
ins	inches
k	knit
k2tog	decrease by knitting 2 stitches together
ktbl	knit through the back of loop
kwise	knit wise by knitting
LH	left hand
mb	make bobble
meas	measures
MC	main colour
M1 left leaning	With your LH needle pick up the bar between your stitches from front to back then knit into the back of it.
M1 right leaning	With your LH needle pick up the bar between your stitches from back to front then knit into the front of it.
p	purl
patt	pattern
p2tog	purl 2 together
p2togtbl	purl 2 stitches together through the back of loop
pm	place marker
ptbl	purl through back loop
psso	pass slipped stitch over
pwise	purl wise by purling
rep	repeat
RH	right hand
rnd	round
RS	right side
Sl	slip
sl st	slip stitch
s2kpo	slip 2 stitches, k1 st, pass the slipped stitches over

ssk	slip next 2 stitches kwise onto the RH needle, slip them back onto the LH needle and knit together through the back.
st(s)	stitch(es)
st st	stocking stitch
tog	together
WS	wrong side
wyif	with yarn in front
wyib	with yarn in behind (at the back of work)
YF	yarn forward

2/2LC (2 over 2 left cross): slip 2 sts from cable needle and hold in front, k2, k2 from cable needle

2/2RC (2over 2 right cross): slip 2sts from cable needle and hold in back, k2, k2 from cable needle

2/2LPC (2 over 2 purl left cross): slip 2 sts to cable needle and hold in front, p2, then k2 from cable needle

2/2RPC (2over 2 purl right cross):slip 2 sts to cable needle and hold to back, k2 then p2 from cable needle

*	work instructions immediately following *, then rep. as directed.
( )	rep instructions inside brackets as many times as instructed

YARNS

All the yarns used in this book are as follows and were supplied by:

Rowan Yarns
Green Lane Mill
Holmfirth
West Yorkshire
UK HD9 2DX
Tel: +44 (0)1484 681881
mail@knitrowan.com

PALETTE A
Ivory 101: white
Moonstone 112: 40k
Black 109: 100k

PALETTE B
Navy 149: 60c, 45m, 35k
Periwinkle 146: 73c, 31m
Ocean 145: 39c, 11k

PALETTE C
Damson 150: 51c, 75m, 31k
Rosy 115: 15c, 45m, 10k
Splash 114: 25c, 35m

PALETTE D
Oxygen 137: 20c, 10y
Azure 138: 60c, 10y
Mallard 144: 90c, 20y, 10k

PALETTE E
Hawthorn 141: 79c, 45y, 49k

Apple 129: 61c, 77y, 15k
Grasshopper 130: 15c, 35y, 9k

PALETTE F
Redcurrant 120: 80m, 15y
Candy 118: 60m, 10y
Pretty Pink 113: 40m, 5y

PALETTE G
Umber 110: 68m, 65y, 80k
Cocoa Bean 105: 40m, 75y, 40k
Almond 103: 7m, 21y, 15k

PALETTE H
Papaya 135: 70m, 40y
Gold 133: 30m, 50y, 10k
Mustard 131: 5c, 5m, 60y, 10k

INDEX

ACKNOWLEDGEMENTS

Geometric Knitting has been one of the most technically demanding books I have ever written and designed. I have loved every minute and it has been an absolute delight and pleasure due mainly to the help of the other wonderful creative people involved.

Thanks must go to the generous help given by David Macleod from Rowan Yarns who helped majorly with the supply of the 24 colour palette used in this book.

My sample knitters have also been tested to the full and have done marvels.

Big shout out to Ann Salisbury, Rita Taylor, Hilary Grundy and Elly Doyle. You have all taught me so much.

Debbie Abrahams supplied the yummy beads suggested for some of the swatches.

Much love also goes to my long-suffering family who put up with late supper, time and time again while waiting for me to finish yet another row or sort out another technical hitch. You might not understand but you give me space to do the thing I love best.

Thank you xxx